1984
AND AFTER

1984
AND AFTER

EDITED BY MARSHA HEWITT AND
DIMITRIOS I. ROUSSOPOULOS

Copyright 1984©

BLACK ROSE BOOKS LTD.

No part of this book may be reproduced or transmitted in any form by means electronic or mechanical, including photocopying and recording, or by any information storage or retrieval system, without written permission from the publisher, except for brief passages quoted by a reviewer in a newspaper or magazine.

BLACK ROSE BOOKS No. M. 84

Paperback ISBN: 0-920057-29-2
Hardcover ISBN: 0-920057-28-4

Canadian Cataloguing in Publication Data

Main entry under title:
    1984 and After

ISBN 0-920057-28-4 (bound).   ISBN 0-920057-29-2 (pbk.).

1. History, Modern — 1945-   — Addresses, essays, lectures.
2. Authoritarianism — Addresses, essays, lectures.
I. Hewitt, Marsha, 1948-   II. Roussopoulos, Dimitrios I.

HN27.N55 1984   909.82'8   C84-090210-7

---

cover design: John W. Stewart
BLACK ROSE BOOKS LTD.
3981 Boulevard St. Laurent,
Montréal H2W 1Y5, Québec, Canada.

Printed and bound in Québec, Canada

Table of Contents

Introduction .... page 9

"1984" and the Specter of Dememorization
       by **Murray Bookchin** .... page 19

Giant Economy Size Brother
       by **John P. Clark** .... page 38

1984: Orwell's and Ours
       by **Noam Chomsky** .... page 66

Prisons: 1984 and After
       by **Claire Culhane** .... page 74

New Forms of Resistance
       by **Yolande Cohen** .... page 98

The Totality of Totalitarianism
       by **Jean-Pierre Deslauriers** .... page 105

Critical Dimensions of Orwell's Thought
       by **Jean Ellezam** .... page 125

Orwell and Anarchy in 1984
       by **Frank Harrison** .... page 143

Authoritarian Education
       by **Robert Mayo** .... page 171

The Real Rocky Horror Picture Show: State and Politics
       by **Stephen Schecter** .... page 192

Job's Comfort: The State and the Arts
in 1984
by George Woodcock .... page 214

About the Contributors .... page 233

Introduction

The occasion of this book is the year 1984. Thirty-six years ago, George Orwell wrote the novel *1984,* which some critics view as a story of futuristic prediction, while others read it as a chilling allegory about totalitarianism in the Soviet Union. A great deal has been published on Orwell's *1984,* so that readers all too familiar with this material might well pose the question: why another book on *1984?* It is not that there is necessarily *more* to be said on the subject, but rather that there is still something *different* to be said, that must be said now more than ever — a perspective, a point of view on Orwell's vision that has not yet been presented.

Those critics who see in *1984* a decisive condemnation of the totalitarian regime of the Soviet Union assume that Orwell's implied intention was a celebration of liberal democracy. The assumption is that Orwell focused his critical analysis outside his own society. Most critics, be they of a liberal, conservative or Marxist stripe, have not sufficiently taken notice of the fact that Orwell's *1984* might well reflect something particularly insightful of the nature of Western society. To understand *1984* strictly in terms of the Soviet Union is very limited; it is now all too apparent how deadly that kind of approach has become. It is also beside the point.

Politically, George Orwell was independent. He was concerned, above all, with what was most fair and just in any particular situation. His essays reflect a basically humanist sensibility which was inclined to take the side of ordinary people in a way that attempted to grasp the reality of their lived experience. When Orwell wrote about coal miners, his sympathy was based upon a first hand experience of what it might be like to actually *be* a coal miner. He did not write about their conditions from a remote, intellectual point of view, but cared enough to go out and live with them in their houses and go down the mines with them. Only in this way was he able to grasp something of their experience as human beings.

He also fought in the Spanish Civil War. It was there that he developed a strong sympathy for anarchism, but this is a fact that many of his critics who are concerned with his politics do not seem to realize. It is important to understand this aspect of Orwell if we are to see the implications of *1984*. If his classic *Homage to Catalonia* was as written about as his other work, this part of Orwell's thought which reflects a profound anti-authoritarian critique would be more widely known. What Orwell shares with anarchism in the novel *1984* is a particular understanding of the meaning of power in the form of a centralized, authoritarian force which destroys everything that is human. The purpose of the present volume is to look at *1984* and the year 1984 from this shared perspective and to see especially how the novel provides us with a set of lenses through which to examine authoritarianism in Western society. If we are successful in fulfilling our goal, this book will then say something about Orwell that has not been said elsewhere.

The contributors to this volume have in common that they are anarchists *and* North Americans. As anarchists they have developed a particular analysis of Orwell's work that is a more sympathetic and accurate reflection of his views, particularly as embodied in *1984*. As North American anarchists, these writers, working in the context of the most technologically advanced, affluent and consumerist society in the world, see that the total administration and domination of civil society that is an accomplished reality in Orwell's *1984*. Surely, one might say, we in North America enjoy the greatest possible freedom ever known in History, and one might well be tempted to conjure up the spectre of a Soviet Union which certainly corresponds much more closely to Oceania than North America ever could. We challenge this widely held view on the grounds that it is a superficial reading of both *1984* and our present socio-political reality. We are not interested in shallow comparisons between Orwell's novel and our society which simply indulge in cataloguing a direct correspondence of leitmotifs. In other words, our main concern is *not* in identifying Big Brother as a not-so-thinly veiled Joseph Stalin. We are interested in *1984* for the way in which it reveals insights into the connections between our social reality and the nightmare world that Orwell described. We are attempting to expose those elements and tendencies in our society which, if left unrecognized and unchecked, could well develop into a society as terrifying as Oceania.

What form might that nightmare take in the West? *1984* presents an important clue in formulating one possible picture. The main theme of *1984* is power in its most brutal form, as dramatized in that chilling scene toward the end of the novel where O'Brien sums up the future for Winston in a single vivid and appalling image:

'But always — do not forget this, Winston — always there will be the intoxication of power, constantly increasing and constantly growing subtler. Always, at every moment, there will be the thrill of victory, the sensation of trampling on an enemy who is helpless. If you want a picture of the future, imagine a boot stamping on a human face — forever.'

If we are interested in what insights *1984* has to offer into the future of our own society, this particular image is perhaps not the most appropriate. It is too strikingly physical, too simple, too direct to provide an image of where we are going in the West. Most people do not yet experience the increasing (and increasingly alarming) encroachment of centralized administration over all aspects of social and personal life that is now taking place, in such direct terms.

The invasion of centralized control over all facets of existence is to some extent hidden in the West. Along with the growing centralization of political power is a more insidious effort to transform human consciousness in order to make it more accomodating and accepting of domination as a natural, if not inevitable, state of things. If one thinks that domination and submission are necessary for social stability, if one accepts the need for a hierarchical authority, it is unlikely that one will experience power as an act of violence against one's freedom and personal integrity.

The problem we face in the West is not simply one of competing ideologies. It is not that we need to formulate an alternative ideology to the existing one, which legitimates domination on all social levels. The problem is much more complex than that. What Orwell understood was that the way to total control of society is through the total absorption of the individual, by obliterating critical consciousness, which is after all, the source of individual resistance. As long as Winston was able to remember something of his childhood and the revolution, or who in fact Oceania was at war with, he was able to resist the Party, he was able to live his own life to some small extent. He could also recognize the lies in the Party propaganda. The Party had not yet been able to penetrate his consciousness completely, and Winston knew the difference between ignorance and strength, freedom and slavery, war and peace.

For its domination of society to be successful, the Party had to annihilate the individual's capacity to think, to make distinctions between concepts, so that one would be unaware of the very existence of the boot that stamps on the human face. There are certain facts, certain realities the Party did not want people to recognize, for example that two plus two make four. An analogous situation that pertains to North America is the Viet Nam war; consider how the people of North America were not supposed to think that the U.S. had 'invaded' Viet Nam, as Noam Chomsky argues in an essay that follows. He tells us that in not 'thinking' in terms of an American invasion of Viet Nam, the American people could not properly grasp the meaning of that war, because the conceptual framework of the collecctive understanding was distorted from the outset with the *a priori* exclusion of an American invasion and aggression in Viet Nam.

This is what *1984* is really about: the disappearance of that critical consciousness which allows an individual or society to discern differences, or to make critical comparisons and find alternatives. The fact that Winston could still think in this way allowed him to resist. Thus, the most crucial scene in the novel that demonstrates domination on the level of interiority is not the scene between Winston and O'Brien, but between Winston and Syme. Syme is working on the definitive edition of the Newspeak dictionary. Syme's job is not to *create* new words for the dictionary, but to *destroy* as many existing words as possible: "We're destroying words — scores of them, hundreds of them, everyday. We're cutting the language down to the bone."

In dismantling language, Syme realizes that to achieve a totally administered society, critical thought must be obliterated. He tells Winston gleefully: "Don't you see that the whole aim of Newspeak, is to narrow the range of thought?... Every year fewer and fewer words, and the range of consciousness always a little smaller." When words are obliterated, so are the concepts they represent. The ability to think abstractly, the capacity to remember, to anticipate and to make comparisons, to devise alternatives — to think critically in short, the very life of the mind, is to be eradicated. This is the aim of Newspeak, in its ultimate, horrific refinement.

Syme recognizes that political control and coercion by brute force are not enough for complete social control. He knows that someday it will no longer be necessary for the Party to use the crude and unpredictable mechanisms of terror and torture in order to achieve total control. The totally administered society will not require such primitive methods because the people will have no concept of anything other than what is. "Even the literature of the Party will change. How could you have a slogan like 'freedom is slavery' when the concept of freedom has been abolished?... there will *be* no thought as we understand it now. Orthodoxy means not thinking — not needing to think. Orthodoxy is unconsciousness."

If *1984* has anything to say to us now, in *our* 1984, it is contained here in Syme's remarks to Winston. The collapse of Western society into total administration by a highly centralized technocratic State will be achieved when the individual and social capacity for self-reflexive, critical thought is finally destroyed. It is not only the patriotic hearts that the State seeks to possess, but also the minds of its population.

What Western society lacks is the *self-conscious recognition* of its own unfreedom and implicit authoritarianism. Whatever recognition there is, is diminishing; yet authoritarianism is increasing, although it has always been there. Our various social institutions — governments, schools, families — teach us that we are free, so that we do not learn to perceive the limitations of our freedom in the existence of domination and control. Yet what is it that children are taught as soon as they are born, from the family, through the education system and in the work place? They are taught to be respectful of, and to obey authority, *for its own sake.*

Human beings are *socialized* beings, and authority is a crucial mechanism in the socialization process whereby people are trained from infancy to submit to ideas and other people as the means of justifying and perpetuating hierarchy. The primary concern of the major social institutions of western society is to produce authority — responsive human beings. The stability of the present political order depends upon it.

If a person learns, at an early enough age, to wait for permission to speak, to go to the bathroom, to eat, to play — if one learns to tailor all one's needs and desires for self-expression to the commands of an external authority who has the power to punish or reward, then one will learn to accept, for example, brutally high rates of unemployment, or the fact that unfortunate necessity dictates the proliferation and deployment of nuclear weapons. One will also assume the need for a strong, centralized State power to dictate the parameters of daily life, from interpersonal relations to global politics. In spite of the pockets of as yet scattered resistance, most people accept the prefabricated views of reality propagated by specialized authorities, be they governments, scientific "experts" or academic intellectuals.

In this context, submission to authority is irrational. It is a matter of habituation — *thoughtless* habituation — to authority which identifies power over others as an inevitable and probably necessary social and political function. Acceptance of hierarchy and authority is largely understood in Western society as not only natural, but somehow inevitable. People are trained to believe that history is shaped and fashioned by individuals of larger-than-life capacities and magnitude. They are "educated' to be quite unconscious of their own power as agents of history; they learn to forget that history is the result of the activities of all human beings before they have even become conscious of the fact. We have *learned* not to see, and not even to be aware of the fact that we have been taught not to see, not to be fully conscious beings. We have forgotten before we ever knew, and have forgotten we forgot. In schools, in factories, in families, we do not learn that there are alternatives to the present system of power nor anything about the possibilities of freedom.

It is therefore not surprising that in our universities, to the extent that socialist thought and history is studied, the anarchist part of this tradition is ignored. Courses on political theory do not mention the anarchist critique of the State, courses on the history of the labour movement do not mention the anarcho-syndicalist tradition, history courses rarely mention even the existence of the anarchist movement. Where there are exceptions to this state of affairs, anarchism is misunderstood and treated in a pejorative way. However, if anarchist theory and tradition were properly taught in schools, it could provide an important critical tool for analyzing the nature of power in both politics and society as a whole. Unfortunately, the political right, centre and Marxist left collaborate in perpetuating popular misapprehensions of anarchist thought and action.

The exchange between Winston and Syme — the latter for whom language would consist of the most simple signs — reflects Orwell's keen awareness of the intricate interdependence of language and thought, and thus the possibilities of human action. "Orthodoxy is unconsciousness", and that is precisely what O'Brien achieved in the final obliteration of Winston. In the end, two plus two really do make five, absolutely no doubt about it. Unquestioningly, unconsciously, two plus two equal five!

> 'They can't get inside you;' she had said. But they could get inside you. 'What happens to you here is *forever*,' O'Brien had said. That was a true word. There were things, your own acts, from which you could not recover. Something was killed in your breast: burnt out, cauterized out.

In the end, Winston's consciousness, his capacity for independent critical thought that he had hung onto as his only shred of resistance to the Party, is vaporized; he even loves Big Brother. "He had won the victory over himself." Winston no longer has the capacity to remember, to make distinctions, to pose alternatives, even to himself. He no longer has any private thoughts, because he has no words, no concepts by which to express or even think them. In a sense, the image of a "boot stamping on a human face" is no longer applicable since it is no longer necessary to control by force. There is a perfect symmetry of internal and external control in Winston; in fact, control and domination no longer exist as such. In Orwell's future, there is no resistance because there is no awareness of anything to be resisted. Winston is no longer a self-conscious thoughtful subject. He is the man of the future who will survive because he fits perfectly in a totally administered world. Winston has been robbed of all knowledge; he has lost his mind. The final disintegration of Winston shows how the personal and political have become pulverized in the completion of the process of final domination. Winston comes to embrace his destroyer in his utter submission to authority.

It is significant that Orwell paints his picture of the future by centering his story around the individual life of one character. The Party can never fully dominate society while individuals *think* resistance. It is also significant that anarchist thought never loses sight of the importance of the individual, never allowing the individual to be sacrificed for the greater glory of any institution or party. In our view, anarchist analysis is the most appropriate critical tool with the capacity to understand authoritarianism in our society in its more subtle, hidden and seemingly palatable forms. The anarchist tradition has consistently pinpointed the power of domination as the key to individual and social misery. What the anarchist tradition continues to do is to develop its understanding of domination and the ways in which it is being constantly refined in all aspects of modern social life. Orwell's *1984* has some of the same concerns.

The essays in this book represent a stream in contemporary anarchist theory and action. These essays build upon some of the classical and most relevant insights of traditional anarchism which has always focused its critical analysis on such issues as the role of the State in social and individual life, as well as the nature of its supporting institutions, such as prisons and the educational system. Anarchism has always concerned itself with the importance of popular (but flexible) resistance movements and the fact of the inextricable relationship between the personal and political spheres of experience, a fact which most political thinkers and activists overlook. The essays here demonstrate how modern anarchism develops these themes in such a way as to see their relevance to our own society.

In recent years there has been an impressive increase in the quality and quantity of anarchist and libertarian socialist research. In disciplines as diverse as sociology, anthropology, history, political economy, social work and linguistics, individuals' work has shown the increase in the use of an anarchist perspective. The contributors to this book are members of the Anarchos Institute founded in 1982, in order to help establish a network between such individuals and groups who are working in these different domains, developing new ideas. This book is the first to be published from this common intellectual and political effort; others will be forthcoming. Through the Anarchos Institute the results of this collective reflection on the theory and practice of contemporary anarchism will be distributed as widely as possible. This book is one such effort towards this objective.

The Editors

"1984" and the Spectre of Dememorization

by Murray Bookchin

Eyewitnesses of the French Revolution tell us that with the overthrow of Robespierre and the Jacobin Committee of Public Safety, the hated aristocrats who came out of hiding in Paris began to co-opt the very Terror by which they had been terrorized. Not only did they participate in the widespread butchery of their erstwhile persecutors — a second "Reign of Terror" that has received little historical attention — but they adopted much of the costuming and behaviour of their victims. It became chic at parties in Parisian mansions to wear a thin red ribbon around one's neck, roughly at the point where the guillotine's blade severed a family member's head from the body. The smart set of Paris adopted this grisly form of ornamentation with alacrity so that the Terror became the backdrop for its special sexual preferences, not only its special social affiliations. The Terror had not merely ceased to terrorize; it was taken into the ballroom and the boudoir where it neither shocked nor forewarned the French aristocracy of future terrors to come but served to awaken and titillate its jaded senses and proclivity for bad taste.

I tell this story because I fear that George Orwell's compelling dystopian novel, "1984", may well be co-opted by 1984. We are beginning to talk about the book with some of the bad taste that marked the French aristocrats of the late 1790s. Barely a month has passed since the beginning of the year 1984 which brought Orwell's novel to the foreground when the book has again become a "hot number" in our bookstores. Comics of the likes of Steve Martin have caricatured the protagonist of the novel, "Winston Smith," with the vulgarity of an Alvin Toffler and the sensitivity of a Herman Kahn. The anniversary issue of the novel has been regaled with a preface, more properly an inventory, by Walter Cronkite about the dangers that could await us if we ignore the real intent of Orwell — not to predict but to warn. Like many inventories, the one prepared by Cronkite is not without its merits but herein too lurks a danger. If "Big Brother" ever comes to America, I think he will look very much like Mr. Cronkite or "Father News," as he has been called by some critics — the anchorman's anchorman who has done as much as anyone on television to abolish news in any meaningful sense and reduce it to entertainment at best and soap opera at worst.

In a more serious vein, we have another corps of commentators — those who take a special delight in emphasizing how lacking Orwell's book was in predictive value. After all, we are told, we do not have "Big Brother," "Newspeak," and a "Ministry of Truth" in the United States, however critical we may choose to be of the Nixon and Reagan eras. The press and the people can still speak out freely. As Cronkite warns us: look at Khomeini and Iran or the Islamic Jihad, although in all fairness, the Cronkite inventory pinpoints many of the social and technical changes since Orwell completed his novel that have brought us closer to "1984" than we care to admit. "Newspeak" is infiltrating our language at an appalling rate and has been doing so for decades. We have been "liquidating" people since the 1920s (to borrow from the vocabulary of Bolshevism), not massacring them. "Media" has been replacing the word propaganda since the fifties.

Electronics, which acquired its ascendency with World War II radar, is the source of words like "input" as substitute for wisdom, "out-put" as a substitute for expression, "feedback" as a substitute for dialogue, "information" as a substitute for knowledge. Following in the tradition of the advertising industry, we "brainstorm" rather than share our views and the military, of course, has given us such juicy expressions as "sanitizing" for bombing missions and "extreme prejudice" for assassinations.

Orwell has argued his case on this subject well in an appendix to the book. "The purpose of Newspeak was not only to provide a medium of expression for the world-view and mental habits proper to the devotees of Ingsoc" — that is, "English socialism" as the societal system in "Oceania" was called — "but to make all other modes of thought impossible. It was intended that when Newspeak had been adopted once and for all and Oldspeak forgotten, a heretical thought — that is, a thought diverging from the principles of Ingsoc — should be literally unthinkable, at least so far as thought is dependent on words. Its vocabulary was so constructed as to give exact and often very subtle expression to every meaning that a Party member could properly wish to express, while excluding all other meanings and also the possibility of arriving at them by indirect methods. This was done partly by the invention of new words and by stripping such words as remained of unorthodox meanings, and so far as possible of all secondary meanings whatever. To give a single example. The word *free* still existed in Newspeak, but it could only be used in such statements as 'This dog is free from lice' or 'This field is free from weeds.' It could not be used in its old sense of 'politically free' or 'intellectually free,' since political and intellectual freedom no longer existed even as concepts and were therefore of necessity nameless. Quite apart from the suppression of definitely heretical words, reduction of vocabulary was regarded as an end in itself, and no word that could be dispensed with was allowed to survive. Newspeak was designed not to extend but to *diminish* the range of thought, and this purpose was indirectly assisted by cutting the choice of words down to a minimum." To call this passage predictive is an understatement. The process of verbal diminution and denaturing has been more pronounced today than at any time in the history of language, thanks to "businessese," "media" exposure, and a barbarous decline in literature and good writing.

To rescue Orwell's "1984" from liberal chic and a contemporary premium on intellectual simplification, we should deal with what in my opinion constitutes the single most terrifying danger from which all else arises in the novel: the need to abolish memory. It is doubtless important to emphasize the centrality Orwell gives to the self-nourishing quest for power that marked the era of "Ingsoc." Many readers of the novel are too far removed from Orwell's era to realize how unique this emphasis was in 1948, the year when Orwell is said to have completed the work. I say "unique" because I can personally recall how secondary or even naive Orwell's concern with power as an end in itself seemed to Western Marxists for whom the "quest for profit" seemed the more "scientific" and "value-free" expression in our understanding of capitalism. Power as an end in itself — in fact, as a self-generating, evergrowing phenomenon for which "profit" and "accumulation" were means — was basically alien to a socialist body of thought that was inherently authoritarian and economistic in its unspoken presuppositions about capitalism, and, I would add, patriarchal "civilization" over the past six thousand years.

Here, Orwell's socialism veered toward anarchism — however much he disaffiliated himself from anarchist movements in England. In *Homage to Catalonia,* Orwell was to exhibit an unmistakable affinity for the anarchosyndicalist workers of Barcelona who rose up in May, 1937, against Stalinist attempts to eliminate workers' control of industry in this anarchist stronghold. His sympathies for this movement were more visceral than ideological. He hated elitism, particularly among English radical intellectuals. His aversion for hierarchy, for the patronizing hypocrisy of Stalinist writers and poets in their dealings with the "masses," was to assume such acute proportions that he refused to meet with the then Communist poet W.H. Auden and shunted away a Communist visitor to his retreat in the Hebrides during the late forties because he suspected him of being an agent of the British Communist Party.

Trivial as these incidents may seem, we cannot ignore them if we wish to put Orwell's book in its own historical context — that is, bring memory to the service of our discussion. "1984" is a book written by a man who gained his political education in the late 1930s. The era and education it furnished explain much in "1984" that we may, at our own peril, fail to notice. Indeed, certain key features of the book may remain inexplicable to us and, correspondingly, desensitize us to their message. Orwell went to Spain in 1937 as a liberal with mixed impulses rather than clear ideas about the need to defend a vague "underdog" against the trammels of fascism. He left Spain a thoroughly shaken man — not because he suffered in the trenches fighting against the "Right," an ordeal for which he was thoroughly prepared, but because he was hunted down on leave by the "Left," notably the Russian-controlled Communist Party and its Socialist allies. For Orwell had inadvertently joined a quasi-Trotskyist militia group of the POUM — the Workers Party of Marxist Unification — a dissident Catalan leftist organization second in strength only to the Spanish anarchosyndicalists of the CNT and FAI. Orwell, in effect, found himself immersed in the politics of the last of the great classical proletarian revolutions at a time when the Communists had become the most outrageously counter-revolutionary force in the present century. The inversion of history — such that the ideals of a Lenin or a Trotsky had turned into their very opposite — constitute the core of "1984." "Newspeak" and "doublespeak" are the changes in reasoning that form the bases of Orwell's novel. "War Is Peace," "Freedom Is Slavery," "Ignorance Is Strength" are the slogans in "1984" that have their counterpart in such distortions of Hegel and Marx as "War is the midwife of history," "Freedom is the recognition of necessity," "From each according to his ability, to each according to his work," a slogan that grossly distorts the old communist maxim: "to each according to his needs." Self-styled "Democratic Republics" and "Peoples' Democracies" abound in the East and "Comrade" still remains the form of address between party opponents who are mutually faced with a bullet in the back of their head at each other's hands.

Within this context, Orwell saw a betrayal not only of ideology, but of the innermost sense of morality and conscience that gives us personality and identity. What horrified Orwell in this egregious inversion of a libertarian revolution in Spain into a numbing civil war within the larger civil war was the command that Stalinism had developed over the only voice of conscience that could have exposed this mockery — the radical intelligentsia of Europe. From Ernest Hemingway to W.H. Auden, from Diego Rivera to Pablo Picasso, from Henry Wallace to Ernest Bevin — all had united, whether cynically or stupidly, to place the red shroud of Stalinist counterrevolution over the black-and-red coffin of the most advanced revolutionary movement of the past century and the last of the great classical proletarian revolutions.

Orwell had lived the travail of "Winston Smith." In a sense, he had been "Winston Smith." But it was not the NKVD, the hired killers of the Russian secret police, who alone assassinated the libertarian leftists in the towns and cities of revolutionary Spain. The horror of Orwell's situation lay in the fact that it was the prestigious writers, poets, politicians, painters — the image-makers and mind-makers of Western society — who had entered into complicity with these killers and hounded him as well when he tried to expose the reality of the Spanish revolution. These were the men and women who made words, crafted articles and books, produced poems and cinema accounts of the civil war, obscuring the events he had witnessed in Spain. The fascists and the NKVD agents killed the dissident leftists of the revolution, a challenge they were prepared to face and return in kind with their own weapons. The radical intelligentsia subverted the integrity of the revolution and degraded its most precious possession - its morale and social personality. They were personified by "O'Brien," who cynically reshapes the very epistemological apparatus of "Winston Smith," who demands nothing less than credulity for his own professional prowess. The image and mindmakers of the 1930s had turned the power of thought into a limp, powerless thing, leaving the "Winston Smiths" of the world no space in which their personalities, identities, and humanity could secretly retreat.

That Orwell exaggerated the role of the 1930s radical intellectuals is no solace to us nearly two generations later. They themselves were captives to what Trotsky has called "the accomplished fact." Russia was the iconization of communism, the dream given materiality, be it in the form of graven images or territory. It was "present" in the dual sense that it was of the "here and now," not of the past with its defeats or the future with its uncertainties. And it was available for tangible inspection, not speculative theorizing. Critical thought had to be suspended before hard facts. Perhaps almost intuitively, Orwell seemed to sense that this very facticity of utopia was the undoing of the utopian hope, just as a seemingly "realistic" blueprint of utopia in every detail — whether real or imaginary — is inherently dystopian in that it dries up imagination, inspiration, development from past, through present, to future. Finally, the facticity of utopia denies us the sense of contrast that juxtaposes past with present so that we can give critical meaning not only to older and contemporary lifeways, but to future ones as well. The supremacy of "the accomplished fact" over past facts and even present ones is the annihilation of the past and even the present, which is meaningless without the past. The present itself thus becomes a specious "Now," atemporal and ahistorical. It is an eternal "Now" that has no origins, genesis, development, and hence, no sense of direction. Eliminate a sense of direction and you eliminate a sense of potentiality, of possibility, of degrees of self-actualization — and of hope, as Ernst Bloch would have said.

Georges Orwell's "1984" trembles with a fearful sense of this turn in human affairs. Yes, the "Inner Party" he describes in the novel as distinguished from the subservient "Outer Party," seeks power. But it is institutionally anonymous, like the Kafkaesque bureaucrats in Russia who fill offices which have lives of their own over and beyond the lives of the human beings who people them. While the personnel changes, the offices remain. Their wooden and metal chairs enjoy a greater longevity than their human occupants. The eternality of an office is sanctified by the ease with which its occupants can be expunged from the world of the living, their biographies and careers leaving no trace of an individual's existence. If they are removed, they never existed. Dememorization, if I may coin a word, is complete. Hence, what "ought-to-be" is never an issue for intellectual consideration because "what-is" has supremacy over "what-was." The eternality of the "Now" is guaranteed by the denial of potentiality, which, as a source of development, is always involved with history and hence memory. Obliteration of memory is the ultimate violation of humanity's identity and capacity to be purposive, to exercise will and effect change. To lose this capacity in Orwell's eyes is to surrender personality itself, indeed, to surrender one's humanity. Thus it is by no means surprising that Orwell inititially titled his book "The Last Human Being in Europe" before adopting the more fetching "1984."

Most of the political material in "1984" follows from this intuitive, albeit occasionally expressed, fear that existed in Orwell's troubled spirit. The institutional paraphernalia of "1984" like the "telescreen," "Thought Police," "Ministry of Truth," hate sessions, rallies, and perpetual wars parallel features that existed fully or embryonically in the Nazi and Soviet states — the latter, incidentally, more so in basic respects than the former. Hitler normally killed his opponents secretly; Stalin demanded the most degrading "confessions" when he could — or wanted — to obtain them. Abusive as the Nazis were of human history, Stalin literally had it rewritten such as to inflict a terrifying atrocity on humanity's record, particularly Russia's. The figure of "Goldstein" in "1984," so essential to the incarnation of history as evil, is literally Trotsky, whose real name was Bronstein. Even the secret "Brotherhood," a fiction by the late 1940s in Russia, was the Left Opposition of 1925 and its "Book" is a mixture of Trotskyist as well as Orwellian analysis and style. Certainly, many aspects of National Socialism appear in the novel, but they are, to an extent generally unknown today, leavings of early Social-Democratic rituals such as highly staged mass rallies and marches which Hitler was to borrow.

So, too, Orwell draws ideologically and psychologically from Arthur Koestler's *Darkness at Noon*. Rubashov, apparently modelled after the real Bolshevik, Nikolai Bukharin, who was to perish in the Moscow Trials of 1938, reasons himself into complicity with his NKVD interrogator who appeals to his revolutionary commitment. Bukharin's memory and honour, stained as it was by his own role in bringing Stalin to power, almost certainly never believed that the Stalinist dictatorship had any redemptive features such as Koestler's Rubashov seems to have believed. With "Winston Smith," Orwell in fact takes us further than the horrible purge trials of the 1930s and later still further than Koestler. Orwell demands that "Winston Smith" must *believe* that "Big Brother" deserves his unqualified love and, in a reverie that closes the novel, "Smith" must welcome execution — almost piously rather than morally.

I have established some very demanding parameters for appraising the novel "1984" in contrast to the year 1984. I have asked that we take note not only of the institutional parallels that link the two but, more emphatically, the psychological parallels that link them — indeed, the ways in which we experience a real or contrived world. I have sought for the "metaphysics," as it were, that relate the novel "1984" with the year 1984, for it is here that Orwell's dystopian work acquires its most fearsome and deepest relevance for our time.

To be sure, we cannot ignore the institutional parallels. Here, it is worth noting that in Soviet Russia, the cracks in the seam are so significant that dissidence is on the edge of becoming an open event. The public adoration of poet-singers like Vysutsky or scientists like Sokholov are evidence of a deep decay in the political structure of Russian society. Ironically, militant Stalinism still exists in Bulgaria and Rumania, where it threatens to become a family despotism rather than a bureaucratic one. China is still so deeply in transition from the Stalinist-type rule of Mao to a semi-capitalist society that we can hardly say that it is moving into or out of an Orwellian "1984." Iran, to speak frankly, is no more evidence of "1984" than was Japan in the closing years of the Second World War. Militant Islamic movements mix nationalism with medieval fanaticism. They are not the outcome of attempts to industrialize as was the case, in part, of Soviet Russia and China. Where they are dominant, they seem to be fanatical minorities that impose their will on a sceptical, if obedient, majority.

Speaking generally, the loss of historical memory which gave rise to "mind control" in Orwell's "1984" is by no means a reality in these countries. People usually know that they are being duped. They live a vast underground life with its own wealth of contacts, cultural artifacts, books, manuscripts, tape recordings, and radio programmes that are largely impervious to the regime's intervention. Fear governs their behaviour rather than the loss of contrast that comes with dememorization. The essence of "1984" is that the people of "Oceania" do not have fear. Their very mode of reasoning and experiencing precludes fear because the authority of "Big Brother" is constitutive of their personalities. The "proles" who seem immune to the demands of obedience are "free" only in the sense that they are behaviourally impulsive and spontaneous. They don't give a damn about the system because the system simply doesn't give a damn about them. Like the helots of Sparta, they are coerced into work by necessity, not by "love" of the society which exploits them.

Where then shall we look for a society that is highly vulnerable to dememorization with its absorbing commitment to the "Now" and the eternality of the contemporary? Perhaps surprisingly, I wish to suggest that the world which more closely approximates my analysis of Orwell's "1984" is our own western society, indeed, the "Oceania" that provides the geographic locale for the book. Obviously, my concern arises not from a similarity between the institutions of Orwell's dystopia and our own. We in America, for the present and the forseeable future, live in a fairly secure republic, not a totalitarian state. This institutional structure has exhibited historically a surprisingly high degree of stability so that, even if we continue to sophisticate our technical equipment for surveillance and control, it can still constitute a barrier to its usage, if not its development. We can be spied upon, every detail of our lives meticulously recorded, and worse, future generations may be exposed to the blessings of bioengineering and behaviour modification. We have reached into the deepest secrets of matter and life without exhibiting the least evidence that we are morally equipped to deal benignly with this enormous body of knowledge.

Orwell's "1984," however, was written in an era of heaving political instability — an era opened by the First World War which culminated in the fascist period that led to the Second World War. Entire republics and constitutional monarchies were wiped out in a matter of months, no less internally as in the case of Italy, Germany, Austria and Spain, as externally with the takeover of Europe by the Nazis. Such political instability has not recurred in Europe in the past forty years, despite the conflicts in the 1950's between the French Army and the new Gaullist regime during the Algerian crisis.

Which is not to say that major institutional changes are not in the offing in the era that lies ahead. The computer revolution which we face with the possible onset of the so-called "Fifth Generation" of symbolic and knowledge information-processing may well turn the "open societies" of the West into highly authoritarian political systems. Given a computer revolution as sweeping technologically as the turn from hunting-gathering to agriculture, I can see nothing in this change that will leave any social and economic space available for tens of millions of people who still hold jobs in industrial, commercial, and retail establishments. These displaced people would have no room in a cybernated society — and, in time, they would have to be "dealt with." There is perhaps room for a new dystopian novel — if it hasn't been written already — that sees a highly regimented society based on enforced population control, a highly militarized political system, and propaganda paraphernalia that would turn dissidence into the highest of social evils.

Yet the republican framework of the West is not easily changed, particularly in the Anglo-American world, because the power of tradition, the constellation of social and economic relations even in the ruling classes, and the ideological commitment of most sectors of the population to a relatively open society place a burden on those who would change a republican system that is not easily removed. There is still very little likelihood that institutional change will occur with the rapidity that marked the interwar fascist era. In this respect, at least, Orwell's hints at such changes and their tempo reflect more closely his own time rather than ours and could be excessively pessimistic.

Where, then, does the danger of "1984" arise? Probably where this danger is most fundamental: the loss of our historical *memory* and the sense of *contrast* it generates. The "telescreen" is not merely a means of surveillance; it is also a means of experiencing. So, too, is the computer. To say that these electronic devices "condition" the human mind is, in certain respects, an understatement of their more underlying *formative* capabilities. I speak of their capacity to restructure thinking epistemologically so that reason becomes a mere tool for controlling the environment or for survival rather than speculation that is critical, that generalizes from "the facts," that is imaginative in its power to probe, and that is creative and reconstructive. The "telescreen" by its very nature — notably, its one-dimensionality as a series of mere images, its immense power to command judgement or even replace it, its hypnotic hold on the mind and senses — degrades the rational faculty *as such* and reduces it to an instrument for narrow pragmatic ends.

The computer virtually ends thinking as a process and replaces it with the end results of thought as an operationally exogenous phenomenon. The "bottom line" of a computer screen or print-out is the ultimate line of computer usage. Mental operations, in effect, tend to become readouts rather than rational activities. Between premise and conclusion exists a machine that inherently separates what one assumes from what one decides, that is, from a rational judgement that stems from a reasoning *process* with a mental integrity in its own right. Freedom is above all a mode of decision-making that involves dialogue guided by moral canons of right and wrong, good and evil, human and inhuman. When a machine takes over this decision-making process, moral guides disappear even as issues to be evaluated and, with them, the very *concept* of freedom. The "smart computers" that are now on the drawing boards threaten to eliminate democratic decision-making completely and widen the gap between premises and conclusions to a point where premises and conclusions are no longer mental operations in any human or social sense but essentially electronic ones.

The combined effect of electronic media and instruments can be almost physiological in character. The mind, which historically was ascendent because it traced the development of ideas from the first flickerings of insight to their realization in thought, was a *thinking* aspect of personality. It was only as good for speculative purposes as the intellectual processes in which it engaged. Herein lay the highest virtue of freedom — of democracy — namely, that it opened these intellectual processes to critical evaluation by a body politic in a public sphere. The Athenian *polis* was free only insofar as it was guided by *logos,* a Hellenic word that combines reason and speech in one meaning. To "talk out" social problems was the first step toward freedom. Greek democracy simply institutionalized this "talking out" process so that it could be as open as possible. But without the process there was no democracy. When this "talking out" or "reasoning out" process is replaced by a machine and the individual is schooled from the earliest years of life to adapt to its electronic operations, the mind ceases to think and begins merely to register. The mind that merely registers what a machine has electronically elaborated is no more a thinking organ than a photograph is the reality of the object or person it records on paper. Such a mind has no need for history or even memory beyond the trivia that are necessary for it to be mechanically operational. Indeed, memory is a burden. It is distractive, irrelevant, disquieting, and seductive in an environment that demands the mere recording of data. Divested of memory beyond the mere operational demands that are imposed upon it, it becomes mindless of its potentialities, its historical role, its range, and finally its creativity. Indeed, it is mindless of its mindlessness. It becomes that textureless, manipulatable, and banal organ which finally oozes into "Winston Smith's" skull after it has been "sanitized" by "O'Brien" and his aides.

Herein lies an epochal denaturing of reason — of mind — that is almost metaphysical in its thrust. A society that may concomitantly change from an active work force to a thoroughly mechanized one and from a world of rational judgements to the registering of computerized results threatens to reduce the ability to judge and make decisions to complete impotence even before freedom disappears institutionally. If a world like Orwell's "1984" begins to emerge, it will not be because technical devices have achieved mastery over mind, but because mind will have become a technical device. "1984" in this form will not come to us explosively and belligerently, but silently, mindlessly, and insidiously so that we will not even know that we do not know, to rephrase the closing line of Jack London's *Martin Eden*. Our mindlessness will consist in the fact that we do not comprehend the meaning of mind. We will have stepped back on the evolutionary scale to a neurological world where the speculative faculties of the mind will have ceased to function and will be seen, if at all, as the relics of an idiosyncratic stage of organic development.

The book "1984" can be rescued from the deadening effects of the year 1984 and its sequelae only by searching beyond a strictly institutional interpretation of Orwell's dystopia. The critical recovery of history — indeed, of the proximate past in our own century — is a vital moral act of intellectuality and resistance. The past haunts us as the biography of humanity's malevolent behaviour and its sublime cultural achievements. The past, in effect, must become integrated into a "Now" — an otherwise eternal "present" — that threatens to efface history, contrast, and continuity like a social "black hole" that leaves mere nothingness in place of any variegated substantiality. Unfortunately, there is no conventional intellectual domain within which this recovery can be achieved. The high hopes which critical theorists like Horkheimer, Adorno, and Marcuse placed in the university have faded completely. Training is replacing education as surely as the registering of "facts" is replacing experience. The job of recovering humanity's memory and voicing it in the authentic language of wisdom belongs to special and, I fear, marginal forms of human intellectual intercourse — the small study group, the fringe periodical, the affinity group that emphasizes theory as well as practice, the "community of scholars" which Paul Goodman celebrated decades ago in a more felicitous and promising era.

"Punk" nihilism, with its shrill cult of egoism and violence, is merely the other side of official "newspeak," its affirmation as a rebellion against mind, not merely against convention and social conformity. In an era that has made "cultural terrorism" a mere fashion at one extreme and moral philistinism a social straitjacket at the other, it is culture and morality that ultimately suffer and decay. Orwell's "1984" is permeated by a searing horror of both: the self-seeking nihilist and the homogenized mass among whom "Winston Smith" is the "last human being in Europe." That Orwell could have anticipated both social types in a manner that speaks to us four decades after his death is a dystopian coup. The error in "1984" lay in the power he assigned to mere sexuality as a redemptive antidote to the authority of a totally controlled social machine. "Julia," the sexual partner of "Winston Smith," is no less a creature of the machine than "O'Brien" and the "Ministry of Truth." For "Winston Smith" is not only the "last human being" in "1984"; he is the last *intellectual* for whom intellectuality is a moral calling and history an abiding conscience. Save for the waning myth that erotic impulses in themselves contravene regimentation, "Julia" is as mindless and hence as unredeemable as the young "spies" who surface in the book. What she "consumes" is not the subterranean culture that "Ingsoc" has hidden from "Oceania," but its rather meaningless barriers to a fast fuck.

It is "Winston Smith's" intellectuality and moral probity that contravenes authority — his obsession with the "Book" that puts "Julia" to sleep, his perilous attempt to recover the past, his willingness to join the "Brotherhood" and act against "Ingsoc," however absurdly Orwell deals with the immoral demands of "O'Brien." His very existence turns him into a "movement," whether the "Brotherhood" be real or not. Hence, "Winston Smith" becomes the conscience of the book, not merely its protagonist. That he can finally be broken by "O'Brien" is testimony not to the impossibility of perpetuating personality, affinity, critical thought, and action in a completely totalitarian world; it reflects Orwell's own innate pessimism and despair for humanity.

Together with the moral alternative that intellectual and cultural affines can create in recovering the memory of an increasingly ahistorical society, there is the issue of recovering and radicalizing the utopian dimension of its traditional institutions. Here, Orwell's "1984" offers us no insights on which to dwell. The supremacy of "Ingsoc's" institutions — its ministries, police, spies, propaganda, and surveillance paraphernalia — reduce "Winston Smith" to an intellectual and moral monad whose relationships and associations never extend beyond the personal. The protagonist's realm of freedom shrivels to an alcove, a shabby room, or a clearing in a forest. Free space has been so completely effaced by Orwell's image of "Ingsoc" that the very deviance of "Winston Smith" is difficult to understand. There is no public domain whatever in the classical sense of the term, only a mass domain. Hence, Orwell leaves us with no rationale for self-awareness, hatred, pretension, much less opposition.

"Winston Smith" is a wriggling and pathetic aberration, not a logical product of oppression.

The promise of resistance in the year 1984 to the book "1984" lies in the very real contrast that is developing between past and present today: the daydreams of the great "bourgeois" revolutions which were embodied in slogans like "liberty and equality" as distinguished from contemporary demands for passivity and survival. The "1984" that an emerging corporate and cybernetic society presage could be made to choke on the *living* memory of its own utopian origins, on the ideological "surplus" that lured Americans and Europeans to the barricades of the past centuries. At a time when the barricade has become more of a symbol than a bulwark and the red flag is stained more by the blood of its own revolutionary bearers than its reactionary opponents, the fragile but memorable *utopian* dimension of the American and French revolutions (in France, so clearly visible to Kropotkin) are all that ideologically stand between the dissolution of this century into Orwell's account of 1984. Be it "liberty, equality, fraternity" or "life, liberty and the pursuit of happiness," these claims of the early revolutions still maintain a vitality in the hearts of the common man and woman that have never been viewed with anything but cynicism in the bourgeoisie. To explode the democratic and libertarian content of the utopian vision these claims retain from their narrow republican straightjacket and to radicalize their democratic content is at least a minimal responsibility for all antiauthoritarian radicals. Here, the mobilization of the public would be more than a recovery of memory. It would be memory embodied in traditional institutions on a *grassroots* localist level, in founding documents that spoke to human liberty for all the abstractness of their language, in a vast choreography of rights and freedoms that still has living tangibility for the people, however mythic its everyday reality. I speak here of a public memory that lends itself not merely to the conservation of existing libertarian institutions or to new ones that have been developed in municipal movements among the people.

For the present we face a minimal need to rescue memory — not only ideologically but institutionally — for a humanity that confronts ideological annihilation. Once this annihilation is achieved, the very discourse of freedom — its terminology and conceptual framework — will be effaced by the "reduction of vocabulary... as an end in itself." The word "clone" was not invented by the critics of the world depicted in "1984"; it was invented by its architects, notably men and women who are themselves the creatures of their own addiction to the promise of biotechnology and cybernetics. "O'Brien," a cryptic figure to say the least, exhibits a degree of consciousness, will, and cynicism that forms neither part of the book "1984" nor the era 1984. The creatures who are surfacing today like anticipatory bubbles from the stew that Orwell prepared for us, forty years ago, lack not only the consciousness, will, and cynicism exhibited by "O'Brien"; they constitute an emerging elite than even lacks the distance of an "O'Brien" to the creatures of their own making. What makes them so horrible compared to all the elites of the past is not that they drive a particularly potent social machine but that they are integrally and hopelessly part of it.

January 19, 1984.

Note: This essay was delivered as a lecture on Orwell's "1984" at the State University of New York at Platsburgh, New York.

Giant Economy Size Brother

by John P. Clark

Good News From The Free World

According to a Gallup Poll published in February of 1984, few people in Western countries believe that the "grim visions" of Orwell's book "have come true." In a survey taken in six nations, most of his "predictions" were judged *not* to have become reality. At one extreme are the Germans and Swiss, who see little evidence of Orwellian conditions, while a bit more is noticed by the Americans, Canadians, and British. Perhaps not surprisingly, Brazillians are capable of perceiving some signs of the existence of the authoritarian State, but even they are divided on the question of whether such developments have progressed very far. In all countries, the greatest concerns expressed were that government officials achieve luxury at the expense of the majority, and that government snooping threatens personal privacy — hardly an expression of belief that the Totalitarian Nightmare has become reality, or that it is imminent.

The most interesting questions posed in the survey refer to conditions that do, without ambiguity, prevail today. Asked whether the government "uses false words and statistics to hide bad news about the economy and quality of life," only 40% of the Americans, 53% of Canadians, and 57% of the British expressed their awareness of these practices. A mere 12% of the Germans and 13% of the Swiss maintain this minimal contact with reality. Another telling question asked whether "the government urges people to surrender freedom in order to gain greater security." Given that every government *requires* people to surrender freedom in exchange for its brand of "security," a failure to respond positively indicates a remarkable ideological blindness. Yet with the exception of Brazil's 35% (itself astoundingly low), the percentage of people expressing agreement was minuscule (ranging from 6% in Switzerland to 12% in Canada).

Despite all the recent discussion of "1984" and its dangers, if one listens to the public it becomes apparent that there is manifestly a great deal of complacency in the face of a considerable loss of freedom in the contemporary world. Or, this seems to be the case if one looks at people's literal responses. Perhaps the failure to get the correct "Orwellian" answers results from the fact that the major constraints on liberty have not occurred in the classic Orwellian manner.

1984 vs. 1984

While some may lament the recent "misuse" of Orwell's novel in the service of anti-communism, this criticism is misdirected. The inspiration for the work is, above all, Stalinism, and it depicts brilliantly the monstrous character of the totalitarian "socialist" State. Attempts to project the Orwellian model on Western societies, so that virtually everything today takes on an "Orwellian" colouring, are doomed to fatuity. Of course, the West has something to learn from *1984* — it is a great work of literature and helps illumine important realms of human existence. Yet its author makes no attempt to show any universally-fated course of development for all modern societies. Big Brother is a striking symbol of authoritarian rule. Yet he should not be taken as the image of unfreedom in the contemporary Western world. For in fact that world has another despot who is at present a more formidable foe, and who should be feared with greater intensity. In the consumer society — the dominant form of "advanced" society — our Brother is a much more agreeable fellow than was Orwell's. * It is the commodity that rules above all other tyrants (and there *are* others in our oligarchy). In *1984* people could be driven to love Big Brother by the occasional frenzy of orgiastic political rituals. In difficult cases they could be tortured into love. In 1984 (the real one), our Brother has no difficulty in capturing our affection. He is with us always as the ubiquitous object of desire.

The Contemporary Relevance of *1984*

The principal relevance of *1984* today can be summarized in one symbol: "$$$." Anyone with any serious interest in the socio-political implications of the book has been studying such issues for some time. One did not have to wait for the magic year to arrive in order to explore its profundities. Ninety-nine percent of the academics who squeeze each word of the book dry of every ounce of portentiousness have never conceded even a single grudging footnote to Orwell's magnificent political classic *Homage To Catalonia*. But now the word "Orwell" will be immortalized in thousands of résumés.

In the real world the exploitation is even more blatant. According to John Hurt, star of the latest film version of *1984*, "We're moving closer to what it describes." His evidence for this momentous conclusion is far from astounding. "Look," he says, "at the bickering between East and West." (N.B. — in the book the Superpowers were in a state of constant war, so perhaps all can be subsumed under the more general rubric of "bickering"). It matters little whether we are overwhelmed by this *tour de force* of historical analysis. The point is to talk Orwell, talk *1984*, talk Big Brother.

As Hurt remarks acutely, "Orwell is a hot topic."

Needless to say, advertising itself has not failed to make use of "1984" themes in order both to sell products and to promote the ideology of free choice (for as we were told as early as 1970 by Toffler in *Future Shock,* the problem today is not *lack* of choice, but rather the dilemmas of "overchoice" in the affluent society).

An exquisite example of "1984" marketing comes from "United Technologies," who tell us that "Orwell was wrong about technology. Technology has not enslaved us. It has freed us." Orwell overlooked technological progress — in particular, the fact that large, expensive computers would give way to small, accessible machines. He knew nothing of The Chip, which has "made the computer so widespread" that it "removes the fears coming from Orwell's belief that the power of the computer would rest exclusively in the hands of an elite few."

Readers of the book will notice that this is a "belief" of which the "believer" himself was not aware. For in *1984*, information was concentrated not in computers, but rather in "vast repositories where the corrected documents were stored." Yet Orwell must hold this "belief" about computers, since the point of the ad is to show that he was wrong. "The electronic chip has put the power of the computer at the fingertips of anyone who wants to expand the scope and clarity of his thinking."

What is suppressed in this paean to the machine is the vast dimension of unfreedom entailed in such technological development: the workers who must adapt to the computer whatever their "wants" or desires, and no matter how much it routinizes their labour; the students who are compelled to learn to use it by the dictates of school authorities; the unconsciously chosen effects of the technology in reducing the "scope and clarity of thinking." Perhaps above all, this technology threatens autonomy by incorporating people into the technological system as information consumers (and very few are information creators!). Like Orwell's telescreen, the computer cannot be an effective means of control to the extent that it is monopolized by a few. The "network" must cast its net as broadly as possible in order to maximize integration into the system.

"United Technologies" indeed!

An even more blatant exploitation of the "1984" theme is Apple Computers' celebrated ad. In this brief but evocative drama, masses of zombies sit hypnotized before a giant telescreen, immobilized by the dominating image of Big Brother. Suddenly a woman rushes down the centre aisle brandishing a sledge hammer. In a spectacular Olympian gesture of anti-authoritarianism she hurls the hammer across the hall and smashes the screen. The message: We are out of the grip of Big Brother... "Apple Computers".

But why "Apple Computers?" A translation for the literal-minded. The "big names," like IBM, stand for big power, for manipulation and control. The Apple stands for the little guy, for "small is beautiful", for individual freedom. The images of Big Brother and the rebelling individual are thus appropriate. They represent the small and independent entrepreneur against the corporate giant, and personalized technology in opposition to totalitarian megamachines. Whether the company is really more David-than-Goliath-like, whether the machines are really warm and cuddly, is irrelevant. We are given two good symbolic reasons to buy an Apple.

Other symbolic connections are, however, to be avoided. While United Technologies argues that the computer offers us new levels of knowledge, we are presumably not to associate the bite of the Apple with Original Sin and the Fall from Paradise, an event occasioned by a similar promise.

"Who Needs The Thought Police?" Or "What's On Tonight?"

Oceania, the society of *1984* is, in a sense, the direct antithesis of the consumer society of today. It is a society of material scarcity which maintains this condition, not through the ceaseless expansion of demands and desires, but through the planned limitation of supply. The populace is kept dependent by the necessity of abject reliance on the State for basic necessities, and either through the perpetual maintenance of a condition of terror (in the case of the Outer Party), or one of ignorance and disorganization (in the case of the proles). The unsophisticated nature of its social conditioning makes it not surprising that the State would have to resort to terror to maintain order among the party members. And considering the abysmal standard of living provided to the second-class elite, one suspects that it is not only our hero, Winston, but most of his co-workers who also yearn to slit B.B.'s throat.

The ineptness of the rulers is illustrated best by their naive use of the telescreen. It serves primarily as a means of surveillance. While people do watch it, they are controlled not so much by their obsessive attachment to it as by their fear that *it* is constantly watching them. The big hit of every season is "The Hate," a repetitive miniseries which momentarily arouses malevolent passions in this passionless society. The State seems never to have discovered the potential of electronic media for control through positive feelings of attachment and dependence. In fact, the proles, who correspond most closely to the masses of today, are not even required to possess telescreens. As "Mr. Charrington" is able to comment, "I never had one of those things. Too expensive."

B.B., you blew it! The proles definitely revolted in *1985*. No doubt they got pissed off after a bad football match, rampaged through the streets, and slaughtered the entire Inner Party so they could drink wine, not vile Victory Gin, for one delirious night.

In 1984 control is much more effective. The typical American family exercises its freedom of choice by watching over seven hours of television per day, as of 1983. While it took 15 years for viewing to increase from five to six hours, the next increment of an hour took but 11 years. If viewing continues to accelerate at this rate, it will reach 24 hours per day well before the middle of the next century, causing difficulties for other popular activities, like working and shopping.

So effectively have TV images invaded the collective consciousness that characters take on a supernatural, paradigmatic quality. While children were once named after favourite saints, admired historical figures, or beloved relatives, the preferred models are now soap-opera stars. The naming of children has always been a revealing ritual in every culture, showing the society's most deeply-held values and aspirations. Apparently, today's parents desire their daughters to partake of the essential qualities of "Heather" and "Monika" of *General Hospital* and "Tara" of *All my children*.

Media images expand their dominance into every sphere of existence, as the culture of consumption generates a morbid dialectic of dehumanization. On the one hand, it drains life from organic culture and from the person by its substitution of prefabricated images for elaborated forms of life. It creates as the end of all its manipulations a spectral non-person, an *Untermensch* of pure externality, a being defined by images and "life style." On the other hand, it appropriates this very being in its perfection and presents it to the consumer as an idealized image of the present.

Examples of such media heroes are abundant — their number is legion. Perhaps the most appealingly grotesque is rock music star Billy Idol. As his name indicates, he is a demigod, both man (the mundane "Billy") and deity (object of worship — "Idol"), thus allowing both identification with a personality and proper awe in the face of the spectacular. As usual, the imagination reveals more than reason intends, for everyone (presumably even rock fans) knows that an idol is a *false* god. Thus the manifest intention of the ritual is both to worship and to identify with the false. Even more obvious is the significance of "idol" as "image." There is then an ironic progression from the human ("Billy") to its negation by the pure image ("Idol").

The content of the image is no less revealing, for we find in Mr. Idol's presentations a vision of violence, necrophilia, and total alienation. In his video "Dancing With Myself," our hero is left alone in a completely solipsistic world. The only other semi-human images presented are hordes of mangled, decaying creatures attempting to invade his (presumably post-holocaust) citadel, and the silhouette (even more radically diminished image) of a naked, chained woman. In "White Wedding" he brutally forces a wedding ring onto his bride's finger, causing her to bleed. Not surprisingly, Mr. Idol has been attacked for his demeaning depiction of women in his pursuit of striking images. His response to criticism is that his intention is merely to *depict* the exploitation of women. Presumably we are to make the civil libertarian judgment that "depictions" can only edify and enlighten, rather than corrupt and demoralize the viewer.

While it is the *modus operandi* of electronic media to commodify culture, the music video is perhaps the genre which is most advanced in perfecting this process. All values, social, political, moral, or spiritual, are a suitable resource for the creation of stylized images and superficial themes. What was once done with perhaps greatest sophistication in fashion photography is now accomplished with vastly expanded impact on consciousness in videos.

What Is "Truth?"

One of Orwell's most powerful insights is his understanding of the breakdown of the concept of objective truth. It would have been entirely natural to present the leaders of the Inner Party as ideological fanatics who are unconditionally committed to their beliefs and prejudices. By avoiding this option, he made it possible to present them as much more authentic representatives of modern nihilism (and, as Nietzsche pointed out, the modern State is one of history's preeminent expressions of nihilistic will to power). They exhibit in its most extreme form the decomposition of all ideals of truth, justice, and goodness. As O'Brien states, "Reality exists in the human mind and nowhere else." Accordingly, "nothing exists except through human consciousness." All barriers to triumphant subjectivity are eliminated. The ego can therefore assert itself without moral or metaphysical limitation.

The abolition of objective truth, in the sense of objective *value,* is a premise not only of the authoritarian society in which might makes right, but also of the consumerist society, in which the image must be right. The only "objective" world becomes the world of "facts," of "brute matter," and of the processes of production and material transformation — the realm of "necessity," as it has been called. Meaning and value reside in an entirely different sphere, the realm of the relative and subjective. Subjectivity is thus banished from nature, and objectivity from the human spirit.

But objective *value* does not truly disappear. Rather it is retained in a completely alienated form. For the sphere of production includes not only mere material objects, but also commodity-images imbued with intensely experienced value. In so far as these images take on the illusion of objective reality and gain power over the subject, objective value remains in existence, but in an entirely opaque, mystified form. The fetishism of commodities thereby permits the simultaneous disintegration of authentic objective values and domination by illusory objective values.

The Land of Spam

If one were pressed to find a single image for the society of commodity consumption, perhaps the most felicitous choice would be Spam. Spam succeeds in embodying at once the productivist power of material transformation and the consumptionist power of imagination. It is the ultimate symbol of the transformation of natural substance and qualities into artificial material with a fabricated image. So thorough has been its metamorphosis that consumers surveyed have difficulty speculating as to its makeup. No one really knows what it is. It is the closest thing to generic "food," and might easily be taken to be the *materia prima* of the entire universe. As Thales (not to be confused with any computer language THALES) might say, "All is Spam."

Yet it is, in fact, real animal protoplasm that has been transformed into the commodity "Spam." But while Spam arose from the destruction of living animals, it has in turn itself generated its own non-living animal image, "The Spam Animal." This is an image created by the Hormel Company to be loved by consumers, who can then transfer their affection to the product itself. Unfortunately, however, dangers lurk in this seemingly innocuous concept. For as a company executive noted, "If we put too much emphasis on the Spam animal, people will be afraid that we kill it and put it in the can."

Interestingly, there is no anxiety about the possibility that Hormel Co. might be killing actual, real-world animals to put *them* in cans. For not being familiar commodities, these creatures have no place in the consumptionist universe. (Urban children grow up unaware of the fact that meat comes from animals, rather than factories, and the truth never really sinks in).

In the Free Market of Ideas one is not likely to hear "messages" like "Mommy, can I have another glob of reconstituted pigflesh?" "Why, of course, Jason, dear, and wash it down with a big glass of Kemical Kola!" No, the only realistic fear in such a world is that the poor imaginary Spam animal might be put back into the very product that generated it (sent like a Spam to the slaughter, as it were).

But the dialectic of delusion moves one brilliant step forward. Our executive asks, "Remember the 'Pet Rock?' " Of course, we remember, but if not we can always be reminded, for in the universe of images nothing is ever lost. In *1984* the past was obliterated. In 1984 everything goes into the memory banks, since all is potential capital.

The Pet Rock was a pet that was not a pet. Its development is instructive. First moment: *Irony* of a thing lacking all the qualities that make it what it is. Latent signification: the inorganic quality of our world — a petrified pet for plastic people. Second moment: *Humour* of treating a rock like a pet. The rough edges of this rock are rounded off, and absurdity domesticated as a conversation piece. Third moment: *Herd-Instinct,* as the good consumer acquires whatever is seen or talked about. A new contribution to the Gross National Garbage.

How can some elements of this classic fad be recycled for the greater glory of Spam? "We will create a cage for the Spam Animal!" suggests our creative marketing executive. The cage will, of course, be *empty.* The logic is unimpeachable: If the Spam Animal is not in the cage, it cannot be thought of as being slaughtered and put in the can. One can thus safely show one's allegiance to Spam (product loyalty) by exhibiting in one's home the *absence* of the *imaginary* Spam animal.

Lest anyone doubt the persistence of Mind in the land of images, this quadruple negation (which puts to shame the pitiable double negations of ancient dialecticians) is one which can be comprehended by any child today. While it is true that some types of rationality atrophy in consumer society, it is equally true that others flourish extravagantly.

No Orwellian world, this! When confronted with the cage for the non-animal, the Orwellian newspeaker would be speechless, or at best might mutter "Where's the animal?" Today's newsthinker recognizes immediately that the cage is not designed for *animals*.

Sex in the ruins

In Oceania a traditional productivist view of sexuality and reproduction prevails, at least for the party members. Sex is solely for the production of offspring, and is assimilated into the sphere of duty of the State. Desire and pleasure are stigmatized as subversive of the regimentation on which the system depends. Sexual repression performs the important function of capturing instinctual energy, which can then be channelled into authoritarian political hysteria. The process roughly follows Reich's analysis in *The Mass Psychology of Fascism*. In view of the political nature of repression, desired sexual activity becomes an act of rebellion against the State.

The limitations of this theory of repression and its negation were long ago demonstrated in Marcuse's analysis of repressive desublimation. If sexual expression can be redirected according to the requirements of commodity consumption, sexuality can be effectively neutralized as a subversive force. This is what has, in fact, occurred in contemporary society, though to a degree unimagined in Marcuse's discussion. Such a solution is hinted at by Orwell, insofar as the proles are controlled in part by the availability of pornography, prostitution, etc. Yet it is not clear precisely how these controls operate. Presumably, they perform an entirely negative function — draining off instinctual energy which in their case is *not* manipulated politically. But the possibility of using the instincts to better integrate the populace into the system of power is not explored.

In the society of consumption, on the other hand, no resource is left unexploited in the pursuit of capital accumulation. Businessmen can charge the services of prostitutes to their Visa or MasterCard, customers of sexually explicit telephone messages are billed automatically, swingers magazines can cater profitably to a lower-middle class Republican clientelle, and *Playboy, Penthouse* and their ilk have long been established as respectable Big Business.

On the level of the individual there is also an imperative demanding the exploitation of sexuality. "Sex appeal" is essential for the successful marketing of one's personality, "image," and "successful life style." In the world of commodities the self becomes a commodity, and the body becomes highly valued capital. Accumulation of sex appeal requires investment in health clubs, exercise equipment, Jane Fonda workout books, plastic surgery, cosmetics, and a variety of sports and diet doctors. In *1984* Winston looked around the canteen of the Ministry of Truth, and was shocked that everyone was so ugly. In 1984 the society of consumption requires *beautiful* people. To project the correct image, one must possess the right "assets" — calculable in qualities of calf, biceps, thigh, waist, etc. And having developed these qualities, the good consumer can then buy some "designer band-aids" (only "three for 99¢!") These ingenious commodities are designed not to "aid" in healing cuts and scratches, but rather to "aid" in drawing attention to one's most well-developed body parts. The Body Politic may be sick, but the Body Economic thrives!

Crimes against nurture

In the authoritarian society of *1984* the production of children is an obligation to the State, and youth are subjected to rigid discipline and control (membership in the Spies, for example). In the consumptionist society the very production of offspring conficts increasingly with the "independent life-style" (read: dependence on maximized commodity consumption) that is the ideal self-image. The result is a decline in the birth rate, except among the most backward and uneducated, and a tendency to "warehouse" both the very young and the very old in the most efficient, cost-effective manner, resulting in minimal interference with productive and consumptive activity.

The long-term effects of the consignment of young children to commercial day-care centres can only be speculated upon. Presumably, the displacement of much of early-childhood experience from the family to a more depersonalized milieu will have far-reaching implications for the evolution of character-structure. While the decline of the intense relationships of the nuclear family may signal the obsolescence of the patriarchal, authoritarian conditioning excoriated by Reich, it may also mean the decomposition of the developed, complex personality which flowered (however faded the flower may often have been) in the bourgeois epoch.

An index of the callousness of consumer society is the extent of mistreatment — ranging from indifference to needs to cruel and abusive acts — prevailing in institutions like day-care centres. The extreme of ill treatment that can be reached is indicated by the recent, widely-publicized case in Southern California (that Oasis of the Bizarre) in which over 100 children were molested by their caretakers over a period of years. The children were abused in multifarious ways, including being sodomized and used for making pornographic films. Presumably, having exhausted the means of exploiting the children on the premises, the ingenious entrepreneurs offered their adult clients kiddies to-go, taking the children to "health clubs" for the sexual use of customers. The parents of the children involved had no suspicion that any such activities took place, and few seemed disturbed by a regulation that they not visit the centre during the day.

While widely condemned, such an enterprise is a model of the capitalist virtue of maximum exploitation of resources, for it permits: 1) the parents to carry on their functions as commodity-producers and consumers, unhampered by the familial demands; 2) children to begin their lives as commodity consumers by using day-care services; and 3) children to be recycled as sexual commodities as they consume, thus allowing a triple contribution to the GNP.*

Politics, the opiate of the masses; Or, Hart of a heartless world

In Oceania, politics was abolished. In the consumer society politics as authentic participation in civic life is virtually non-existent; yet, the political is retained as an important element of the legitimating process. While the public has long had a dim awareness of the nature of the game, and cynicism continually erodes whatever political faith persists, people still cling tenuously to some remnants of the political illusion.

While the masses' true loyalty is to the commodity and not to the political system, every four years the American State — much like its counterparts elsewhere — takes a new stab at mending its fractured legitimacy. The means, needless to say, is the marketing of a fresh crop of politicians as new, improved

---

* Should we then be opposed to 'day care' as such? We must realize that given the existing social structure it will mean, in general, either the commodification of child care or its absorption into the welfare state bureaucracy. It will be up to liberals to extoll the better day-care centres and to propose reforms of the existing system. The libertarian and communitarian response is to work for its replacement by cooperative child care.

commodities. The latest Grade A product offered to the political consumer is Gary Hart. It is well known that Sen. Hart has attempted to recycle several aspects of the JFK image with moderate success mystique-wise. What is less known is his excellent pedigree of generations of image-consciousness. The Senator's surname originally derived from the family name "Eberhart Penz." This alien, Germanic patronymic was wisely Americanized into the more acceptable "Hartpence." But this was still a somewhat unusual denomination. It remained for Gary himself to take the decisive third step, reducing it to "Hart," a name evoking both a noble beast and the seat of all benevolence within the human person.

It is fitting that someone possessing such originality should base his appeal on his commitment to "new ideas." Sen. Hart assures the public that he has them, and many Hart fans do indeed report that they support him because of these very ideas. His opponents (especially Mr. Mondale, who represents "the traditional Democratic coalition," an old, worn-out, but still useful idea) have not failed to point out that he has yet to reveal the precise content of the ideas, or explain in what sense they are "new." Yet this only shows their hopeless confusion concerning the electoral process or would, if their "analysis" were anything other than (the counter-image that it is). Sen. Hart's "new ideas" in no way signify that he actually possesses specific concepts in his mind that are in some way novel. Rather, they signify that he is to have the *image* of "a person having new ideas" — the question of their existence is at best irrelevant. In fact, the disclosure of truly innovative concepts might make the candidate threatening to large segments of the populace, and would certainly complicate and hinder the process of selling him as a generally consumable product.

Do images have standing?

As political institutions are ever more perfectly absorbed into the spectacle of commodity-consumption, "justice" has its turn to become a media commodity. While courtroom drama has been a media staple since Perry Mason, the exploitation of this theme reached new heights with the introduction of authentic courtroom testimony in the New Bedford "Barroom Gang-Rape Trial." Cable News Network, which presented hour after hour of detailed testimony concerning the rape, solemnly defended its decision to do so, on grounds that it was important to inform the public about this crucial issue. In other words, CNN will present *anything,* no matter how lurid and fascinating, no matter how positive the effect on ratings, so long as it promotes the cause of Good Citizenship.

This profaning of the sacred judiciary did not go uncriticized, albeit confusedly. A professor from the prestigious Annenberg School of Communications proclaimed such phenomena "show trials," and likened them to practices in Stalinist Russia, China, and Iran. Yet this particular Orwellian allusion is misplaced, for the traditional authoritarian function of the cases mentioned is confounded with the consumptionist function of media trials today. The professor confuses the "show trial" of the past with the "trial show" of today.

Decadence hits workers' paradise

While consumptionist values are firmly established in Western societies, they increasingly infect the "Eastern bloc" also as production continues to climb and Western influences maintain their slow but continuous process of infiltration. Symbolic of this historic tendency is the introduction of high fashion modelling in Moscow. Recently, the elite of the State capitalist regime sat back and enjoyed their Vodka Colas, as they were treated to the same parade of ghostly figures that one is accustomed to seeing in New York, Paris, or Milan. While the models went through the same mechanical posturing as do their Western counterparts, the themes differed somewhat. While in New York one can see expensive caricatures of, for example, the Ecuadoran peasant, the Astronaut, or (irony of ironies!) the Bag Lady, the Muscovites were served their own unique brand of cultural vampirism. The big hit of the show followed a Socialist theme: Not Proletarian Realism, however, but rather stylish, and highly stylized outfits based on the Great October Revolution. While it is no secret that the Revolution has long been dead in Russia, such an event indicates a surprising degree of ideological disintegration, and suggests unexpected advancement toward the general substitution of consumptionist values for authoritarian ones.

The People's Republic of China has been no more successful in preventing the return of the repressed commodity. It is no secret that the post-Mao regime is making a concerted effort to incorporate into the socialist system all the advances of Western technological society. Presumably "economics in command" will lead to rapid commodification of the culture. Already the State has begun to build luxury condominiums near Hong Kong, so that rich capitalist executives can commute between the People's Republic and the sweatshops in which they oppress the toiling masses. While this apparent sin against socialist morality can no doubt be explained away in the name of the exigencies of socialist development, the true and mortal sin is the poisoning of the minds of the workers by the spectacle of the "beautiful people" living the "good life."

Another force destined to transform China is the invasion by Western tourists. The People's Republic is now investing in tourism in a big, and often ingenious way. For example, there are two kinds of hotels offered to the Western visitor. One is typified by a newly-built structure we might call the "Running Dog Hilton." A Western-style high-rise luxury hostelry, it is topped by that pinnacle of sophisticated elegance, the revolving lounge. So awe-stricken are the Chinese by this magnificent edifice, that they allegedly photograph themselves with it as a background at all hours of the day.

At the other extreme of tourist accomodations is a complex we might call the "Immiseration Inn," a remodelled commune with just enough comforts of home to make the atmosphere exotic rather than oppressive. Here the visitor can play peasant, inhabiting homely dwellings, taking the oxen for an occasional spin, and even doing a Marie-Antoinette-like stint in the rice paddies.

Even more menacing to the remnants of socialist ideology is the growing interest of Chinese leaders in advertising. As two American advertising executives recently testified: "They *want* to believe in advertising." And, indeed, they should, since 25 years after the Revolution it would be naive to think that a billion people could be kept under control by reciting the various inanities of Mao's *Little Red Book (Little-Read Book?)*. True, the Socialist Leaders still had reservations about the quintessential capitalist techniques of marketing, but their misgivings were rapidly laid to rest. As the executives reported: "They asked us, 'Does advertising lie?' We had great answers and the Chinese accepted them!"

Presumably, elites East and West have found common ground: The truth is what works.

The sick society

In Oceania, "there were fear, hatred, and pain, but not dignity of emotion, no deep or complex sorrows."

Today we find a similar loss of *complexity* of feeling, but with it a loss of the *intensity* of feeling that was retained even in Orwell's dystopia. Instead of fear, hatred, and pain, we increasingly encounter anxiety, annoyance, and malaise. Life is perceived as a burden, but not because of the oppressiveness or injustice of our mode of existence. Rather, the "cost of living" seems too high. "The bottom line" is slightly in the red.

Strangely, as "lifestyle" flourishes, *life* increasingly has less meaning. An epidemic of suicide has broken out, for example, among teenagers, the vanguard of the consumer society. The rate of suicide among the young has increased 50% in only a decade. Especially in suburbia, the most advanced sector of contemporary society, shocking outbreaks appear. In a single Dallas, Texas suburb, seven teenagers killed themselves in a single year. In a northern California suburb the total reached twelve. In one case a child allegedly chose this path as the result of severe depression following the news that he would have to wear braces for several years. Presumably, non-existence was preferable to the projection of an incorrect image. Whether this report is accurate or not, there is certainly a severe crisis resulting from the growth of narcissistic personality structures. Increasing numbers of people are unable to plan for, or even conceive of, a meaningful future that is worth struggling for, and become locked in an eternal present of passive, uncreative consumption.

Much in line with the proliferation of such problems, one popular model of the contemporary world depicts it as "the therapeutic society." This concept contains a partial truth, for many institutions have been transformed according to the therapeutic perspective. Thus, prisons as a means of dispensing retributive justice, or even as pragmatic instruments for "impacting positively" upon "social problems," increasingly give way to therapeutic "treatment" of the maladjusted. This is just one aspect of a generalized trend. As society progressively disintegrates into a collection of atomized, egoistic consumers, every element of the alienated personality spawns hordes of therapeutic experts inundating the public with manuals, guides, tapes, videos, courses, groups, sessions, etc.

All becomes technique. As a "sleep expert" was recently asked by a television interviewer, "Should we regard sleep as a natural function, or as a skill to be learned?" One may indeed wonder.

Yet all is not therapy, and the model in question is a flawed one. Thereapy is just one, albeit pervasive, aspect of the consumptionist and productivist sectors. It is another commodity aimed at satisfying the ever-expanding needs and desires generated by consumer society. Just as every organ, tissue, and even cell of the body must ultimately be exploited by the medical industry, so every dark recess of the psyche must ultimately be exploited by the therapy business. And to the degree that we produce alienated, but at the same time narcissistic and self-indulgent consumers, we create the ideal customers for this growth industry.*

Perhaps the most striking similarity between the society of *1984* and the society of consumption is in the striving of both to eliminate history. In *1984* "history has stopped. Nothing exists except an endless present in which the Party is always right." In 1984 history is indeed coming to an end. This is the imminent fate of Western society and the eventual fate of all that comes under its suzerainty. Beginning with the secularization of the Judeo-Christian eschatological vision, the West has been an historical civilization. Historical time has been the framework in which human destiny has worked itself out, whether this

---

* While psychotherapy will no doubt continue to perform its assigned function in the system of production and consumption, there have been some valiant attempts to uphold the ideal of critical and radical psychoanalysis. For an especially notable example, which includes much brilliant social analysis, see Joel Kovel, *The Age of Desire* (New York, Pantheon 1981).

destiny has been conceived of as the conversion of all nations to Christianity, the triumph of civilization over savagery and barbarism, or the establishment of universal Communism. This historical movement is now being definitively terminated by the expansion of capital to its limits. There is now a consensus in the "developed" world that material production and commodity consumption are the fundamental tasks of humanity (the ultimate "bottom line"). Consequently, there are for the "advanced" societies no transcendent or ideal standards by which to judge historical movement or even the value of particular forms of life. We are left to wait for the dawning realization that under the mask of "economic growth" hides an eternal recurrence of the same. We begin to fall into a new cyclical time lacking the mythic dimension of primitive temporality. We are left in an "endless present" in which not the Party but the Commodity is always right.

The end of humanity?

Perhaps it is not only history but humanity itself that is now dispensable. Presumably, as the self becomes more and more shadowy in a world of images, we can eventually disappear completely. The technology is, in any case, ready to step into the breach. One can imagine the home of the not too distant future. The reassuring sound of the television set drones on, as all the best programmes are faithfully recorded on the VCR machine. The computer terminal is on-line, bringing in all the latest news, in addition to information about sales and specials at leading department stores. Our user-friendly computer is programmed to order automatically key products at preselected prices, and to print-out news items of special interest. The telephone answering machine is always alert, repeating its witty message concerning no one being at home, and taping all the prerecorded calls that increasingly bombard it. All the dials are set, so the washing-machine washes our clothes and the automatic dryer dries them, while the oven — better yet, the radar range — cooks to calculated perfection our pre-packaged, processed and prepared food products. It is, of course, a self-cleaning oven. All the while, the digital clock pulsates facelessly onward.

The end of thinking?

In *1984* Newspeak was created to narrow the range of thought through a continual process of simplification and elimination of vocabulary. Today the range of thought has not so much been narrowed as rechannelled. The language *expands* regularly, above all with technical vocabulary and terminology needed to keep pace with the process of commodity-production. On the other hand, modes of thought and expression at variance with the requirements of technological and consumptionist society begin to disappear. For example, mass-media and the educational system work to dissolve local and cultural diversity, which produce conflict with dominant values. There has thus been a process of homogenization and standardization of thought and language, while at the same time an expansion and diversification has taken place within these limits.

The psychology of belief has changed accordingly. Orwell's Doublethink required a certain quantity of mental discipline, since one was obliged to hold two contradictory opinions which one *knew* to be in conflict. This clarity and willfulness worthy of a Tertullian no longer exists today. While people are expected to accept ideological principles, they are seldom aware of any conflicts between various articles of faith, or between these and other areas of experience. A vague and confused adherence to amorphous beliefs is all that is expected. Furthermore, as the "information society" overwhelms the mind with an endless clutter of disconnected and unanalyzed data, the chance of any particular belief or combination of them becoming a threat to the order of things is increasingly less likely.

The enduring relevance of *1984*

Having said much about the ways in which *1984* does *not* describe contemporary Western society, I feel compelled as I conclude to add a few words concerning the profundity and relevance of the work. My final reference to the book will therefore be to the passage that I believe to be its most brilliant. Near the end of the book O'Brien comments that it is clear enough to everyone *how* the Party rules. The more significant and challenging question is *why*. He poses this question to Winston: "Why should we want power?" Winston replies that "You are ruling for our own good... You believe that human beings are not fit to govern themselves, and therefore —", at which point he is administered an excruciatingly intense shock for having given such a ridiculous answer.

As O'Brien explains, "The Party seeks power entirely for its own sake." What is desired is not merely any kind of power, but "pure power." A contradiction is encountered in the individual's search for power, for the quest is doomed to end in failure. All human beings will weaken, die, decay. The entire undertaking therefore seems futile. But if one can "make complete, utter subjugation, if he can escape from his indentity, if he can merge himself in the Party so that he *is* the Party, then he is all-powerful and immortal." Power can once more have meaning, especially insofar as its truest form is attained — not mere power over matter, "but, above all, over the mind."

Orwell thus gives us a perceptive insight into the psychology of authoritarianism, but even more importantly, he touches on some universal aspects of modern humanity. Indeed, he is hinting at some essential qualities of civilization itself. For if in authoritarian society the elite are driven by the quest for a power which raises them above their limitations and mortality, this is no more than a striving that is identical with the history of civilization. It is equally the truth of the society of consumption. The commodities which become the *raison d'être* of the person as consumer are not mere objects, but images also. The consumer does not only buy a collection of products, but also a constellation of commodity-images constituting an imagined self. While society is rather frank in admitting that to be successful one must "sell oneself," it has been less explicit in stating the corollary: that one must also buy oneself. Yet everyone knows that this is true. In consumer society one does not have to dominate in the style of an authoritarian elite in order to exercise significant power. Instead, one may invest in the production of the correct self-image and successfully sell it to others. Given the multitude of levels of status within the technobureaucratic system and the extensive and ambiguous hierarchy of commodities, one has enormous possibilities for relative success or failure in image-credibility. The promise of the society is, though, that to the extent that one succeeds in this endeavor, one rises above mundane existence — "everydayness" — and achieves a kind of idealized Being. Consequently, it is possible to escape, however precariously, from mortality and the limitations of the actually existing self. The entire project is fraudulent, but it is no more fraudulent than the identification of the self with the authoritarian state or party that Orwell describes. In both cases there is a denial of reality in the pursuit of recognition by self and others — of "power over mind."

The end of civilization

Our theme has been the dominant position of consumptionism in contemporary advanced capitalist society. While Big Brother stands in the wings, ever ready to apply the electrodes, at centre stage in today's spectacle of power is our Giant Economy Size Brother, the commodity. There is a danger that one might infer that since ideological control is so powerful today there is even less opportunity for escape from our Brother than from Orwell's. This is not necessarily the case.

First, it must be recognized that consumptionism has in fact challenged the traditional authoritarian structure of society. To the extent that productivist society in its classical period laboured under the yoke of the performance principle, we have gained a degree of freedom with the deterioration of this principle. Thus far the consequences of this freedom have been deeply disturbing (as I have stressed in this discussion), linked as they have been to the dissolution of the organic fabric of society. As Janis Joplin so aptly pointed out, freedom can be "just another word for nothing left to lose."

Yet, there are two moments in the development of contemporary culture, and the fulfillment of each is a real historical possibility. On the one hand, there is the obsessive consumption that has been described here, an endless striving toward an elusive fulfillment, the progressive destruction of all existing values in the name of a dream that is incapable of definition. But this quest is doomed to failure. It can only lead to a spiritual immiseration less bearable than the material immiseration of the early industrial era. The true crisis of capitalism (in both its corporate and Statist varieties) is a crisis of the spirit.

The impasse confronting consumptionism creates hope that the way will open for the unfolding of another moment of consumptionist society — the submerged utopian moment whose fate lies with the radical imagination. To the extent that the imagination has unbound itself from its subservience to the commodity, it has engendered a vision of completeness, happiness, fulfillment, self-realization, and reconciliation. With the dissolution of the authoritarian structure of productivist society, civilized humanity can for the first time dream of wholeness — or, to speak more accurately, allow the dream to make its way into consciousness.

The fate of this vision rests with our success in reconciling imagination with theoretical and practical reason, that is, with a new understanding of humanity and nature, and a new practice of liberatory social transformation. If this can be achieved, then, when the dialectic of civilization has finally played itself out, disinherited humanity may finally awaken to the abyss in which it has been falling. And, in the face of the void, it may then take up in earnest its quest for a plenitude of being.

NOTE

* The identification of contemporary society as "consumer society" or "consumptionist society" indicates its most salient characteristic and points out the direction of its movement. Yet this is a vast oversimplification of a complex system. On the most general level, it underemphasizes the centrality of the technological and political spheres, which are profoundly conditioned by commodification, but remain irreducible. Furthermore, consumption is itself dependent on the realm of production, so that the "economic" (even in its expanded sense implied here) contains mutually interdependent, dialectically interacting productivist and consumptionist sectors, with corresponding productivist and consumptionist ideologies.

    One of the most significant facts about contemporary society is that while these two realms are interdependent, an increasing degree of contradiction between them is developing, especially as consumptionism becomes the far more powerful ideology and its values begin to invade even the most classically productivist institutions. Thus, the famed "revolt against work." Yet one should not rashly conclude that one has discovered fatal contradictions in the system, especially when these depend on largely unconscious and instinctive activity. The consumptionist desire for gratification does not necessarily lead to a *rejection* of alienated labour, merely displeasure with it. Most good consumers recognize that they must (so they think) subject themselves to mindless toil if they are to consume at a satisfactory level. Perhaps what is undermined most by consumptionism is not the capacity to engage in meaningless labour, but rather the capacity to engage in *meaningful labour*. Once intrinsic goodness is drained from production, only enforced labour is possible. The consumer submits him or herself to more or less regimented work out of a necessity for "survival" (i.e., survival as a commodity consumer, rather than existence in any other mode of being). Beyond this, only the passivity of consumption is conceivable. When called upon for more creative activity (voluntary association, political activism, etc.) the alibi is that all one's "energy" is wasted in the pursuit of "survival", when, in fact, it is all one's *imagination* that is depleted. (For a more extensive discussion of productivism, consumptionism, and their possible contradictions, see "The Labyrinth of Power and the Hall of Mirrors" in *The Anarchist Moment* (Montréal: Black Rose Books, 1984).

As is hinted at later in this discussion, the possibility of liberatory social transformation depends finally on the growth of critical consciousness of the ways in which both productivism and consumptionism brutally cut off the opportunities for humanity and nature to achieve a process of non-dominating self-realization. This consciousness depends, in turn, on an understanding of the meaning of the good in relation to human nature and the cosmos. (I take up this issue in "On Taoism and Politics" in the *Journal of Chinese Philosophy,* Vol. 10, no. 1, reprinted in *The Anarchist Moment*).

1984: Orwell's and Ours

by Noam Chomsky

Last May, a remarkable event took place in Moscow. A courageous newcaster, Vladimir Danchev, denounced the Russian war in Afghanistan over Moscow radio in five broadcasts extending over a week, calling on the rebels "not to lay down their arms" and to fight against the Soviet "invasion" of their country. The Western press was overwhelmed with admiration for his startling departure from «the official Soviet propaganda line.» In the *New York Times,* one commentator wrote that Danchev had "revolted against the standards of double-think and newspeak." In Paris, a prize was established in his honour to be given to "a journalist who fights for the right to be informed." In December, Danchev returned to work after psychiatric treatment. A Russian official was quoted as saying: "He was not punished, because a sick man cannot be punished."

The event was considered to have afforded a glimpse into the world of 1984, and Danchev's act was justly regarded as a triumph of the human spirit, a refusal to be cowed by totalitarian violence.

What was remarkable about Danchev's action was not merely the protest, but the fact that he referred to the Russian invasion of Afghanistan as "an invasion." In Soviet theology, there is no such event as "the Russian invasion of Afghanistan." Rather, there is a "Soviet defense of Afghanistan" against bandits supported from abroad. As in the case of most propaganda systems, here too there is a kernel of truth concealed in a massive lie. The Mujahidin do operate from "sanctuaries" in Pakistan, where CIA and Chinese agents oversee the flow of arms, and the guerrillas take credit for having destroyed 50% of all schools and hospitals along with many other acts regarded as "atrocities" by the invaders, who have stated that they will withdraw if Afghanistan is secured from attack from Pakistan. This stance is dismissed by the West on the proper grounds that aggressors should withdraw "unconditionally," as the UN Security Council insisted, with US support that was quickly withdrawn, in the case of Israel's invasion of Lebanon. The West has also been justly indignant when the Russians cynically denounce the "terrorism" of the resistance, or when they claim, absurdly, to be defending Afghanistan from these "bandits" who murder innocents.

The USSR protests that it was invited in, but as the London *Economist* grandly proclaimed, "an invader is an invader unless invited in by a government with some claim to legitimacy." Only in Orwellian Newspeak can such aggression be characterized as "defense agsinst externally-supported terrorism."

Orwell's *1984* was largely drawn from the practice of *existing* Soviet society, which had been portrayed with great accuracy by Maximov, Souvarine, Beck and Godin, and many others. It was only in cultural backwaters such as Paris that the facts were long denied, so that Khrushchev's revelations and later Solzhenitsyn's reiteration of the familiar story came as such a revelation at a time when the intelligentsia were prepared to march in a different parade. What was striking about Orwell's vision was not his portrayal of existing totalitarianism, but his warning that it could happen here.

So far, at least, that has not come to pass. Industrial capitalist societies bear little resemblance to Orwell's Oceania — though the terror-and-torture regimes they have imposed and maintained elsewhere achieve levels of violence that Orwell never depicted, Central America being only the most obvious current case.

Implicit in the press coverage of the Danchev affair was a note of self-congratulation: it couldn't happen here. Here, it requires little courage to defy the government on a point of doctrine. Certainly no Danchev has been sent to a psychiatric hospital for calling an invasion an "invasion." But let us inquire further into just why this is the case. One possibility is that the question does not arise because, statistical error aside, there are simply no Danchevs here: journalists and other intellectuals are so subservient to the doctrinal system that they cannot even perceive that "an invader is an invader unless invited in by a government with a claim to legitimacy," when it is the US that is the invader. This would be a stage beyond what Orwell imagined, a stage beyond what Soviet totalitarianism has achieved. Is this merely an abstract possibility, or is it an uncomfortably close assessment of our own world?

Consider the following facts. In 1962, the US Air Force began its direct attacks against the rural population of South Vietnam, with heavy bombing and defoliation, as part of a programme intended to drive millions of people into camps where, surrounded by barbed wire and armed guards, they would be "protected" from the guerrillas they were supporting, the "Vietcong," the southern branch of the former anti-French resistance (the Vietminh). This is what we call "aggression," "an invasion," when conducted by some official enemy. The GVN had no legitimacy and little popular support, and in fact its leadership was regularly overthrown in US-backed coups when it was feared that they might arrange a settlement with the South Vietnamese enemy. Some 70,000 "Vietcong" had already been killed in a US-directed terror campaign before the outright US invasion in 1962. The US invaders continued to block all attempts at political settlement, and in 1964 began preparations for a vast escalation of the war against the south combined with an attack against North Vietnam, Laos and later also Cambodia.

For the past 22 years, I have searched in vain for even a single reference in mainstream journalism or scholarship to an "American invasion of South Vietnam," or American "aggression" in South Vietnam. In the American doctrinal system, there is no such event. There is no Danchev, though in this case it took no courage to tell the truth, merely honesty. Even at the peak of opposition to the US war, only a minuscule portion of the articulate intelligentsia opposed the war on grounds of principle — on the grounds that aggression is wrong — while most came to oppose it, well after leading business circles did, on the "pragmatic" grounds that the costs were too high. Popular attitudes, incidentally, were rather different. As late as 1982, over 70% of the population (but far fewer "opinion leaders") regarded the war not just as a mistake, but as "fundamentally and morally wrong," a problem known as "the Vietnam syndrome" in American political discourse.

These facts should give us pause. How was such astonishing subservience to the doctrinal system achieved? We can begin to understand by looking more closely at the debate in mainstream circles between the "hawks" and the "doves". The hawks were those, like journalist Joseph Alsop, who felt that with sufficient dedication the war could be won. The doves agreed with liberal historian Arthur Schlesinger that it probably could not, though like him, they took for granted that "we all pray that Mr. Alsop will be right." It was a "hopeless cause," as critic Anthony Lake recently observed. All agree that it was "a failed crusade" undertaken for motives that were "noble" though "illusory" and with "the loftiest intentions," in the words of Stanley Karnow in his recent bestselling history, highly regarded for its critical candour.

Strikingly omitted from the debate is the view that the US could have won, but that it would have been wrong to allow aggression and massacre to succeed.

This was the position of the authentic peace movement (if the war was a "hopeless cause," why bother to protest and disrupt it, why suffer the consequences of that protest, which were often severe?).

This quite typical commentary illustrates the genius of "brainwashing under freedom." In a totalitarian system, it is required only that official doctrine be obeyed. In the democratic systems of thought control, it is deemed necessary to take over the entire spectrum of discussion: nothing must remain thinkable apart from the Party Line. State propaganda is often not expressed, merely presupposed as the framework for discussion among right-minded people. The debate, therefore, must be between the "doves" and "hawks", the Schlesingers and the Alsops. The position that the US is engaged in aggression, and that such aggression is wrong, must remain unthinkable and unexpressed, with reference to the Holy State. The "responsible critics" make an estimable contribution to this cause, which is why they are tolerated, indeed honoured.

The nature of Western systems of indoctrination was not perceived by Orwell and is typically not understood by dictators, who fail to comprehend the utility for propaganda of a critical stance that incorporates the basic assumptions of official doctrine and thereby marginalizes authentic and rational critical discussion, which must be blocked. There is rarely any departure from this pattern. Perhaps the sharpest critic of the American war in mainstream journalism was Anthony Lewis, who argued that the US involvement began with "blundering efforts to do good" but by 1969, it was clear that it was "a disastrous mistake." Few academic scholars were more critical of US policy than John K. Fairbank, who informed the American Historical Society in his December 1968 presidential address, a year after the Tet offensive had convinced much of the corporate elite to abandon the effort to subjugate South Vietnam, that we entered the war in an "excess of righteousness and disinterested benevolence," but it was a mistake to do so, as events showed. Few dictators can boast such total conformity to Higher Truths.

The devices that are used to ensure such obedience are effective though not overly subtle. Consider, for example, what is universally called the "peace process" in the Middle East: the Camp David accords of 1978-9. Few ask why the inhabitants of the territories under Israeli occupation reject the "peace process" with virtual unanimity. A moment's thought suffices to provide the reason. As was obvious at once, the "peace process" served to remove Egypt from the conflict so that Israel would then be free, with US support, to extend its settlement and repression in the occupied territories and attack Lebanon, exactly as it has been doing since. But such elementary observations are excluded from "responsible" discussion: the US is committed to the creation of a powerful and expansionist Israel as a "strategic asset". Anything that contributes to this end is, by definition, the "peace process." The term itself eliminates any further discussion: who can be against peace?

There are thousands of similar examples. The US marines in Lebanon are the "peace-keeping force", and actions taken against them are "terrorism." For much of the population, they are simply consummating the Israeli invasion with its "new order": the rule of right-wing Christians and privileged Muslim sectors over the poor and disadvantaged whose "terrorism" in their own eyes is resistance, a point of view excluded from discussion here. When Israel bombs villages near Baalbek with 500 casualties, mostly civilians, including 150 schoolchildren, that is not "terrorism" but "retaliation," and it receives no comment or censure here: as an American ally, Israel inherits the right of aggression and massacre. Often, unwanted facts are simply suppressed. The "secret bombings" of Laos and Cambodia were "secret" because the media refused to report the ample evidence available. The US-backed Indonesian aggression in Timor, leading to the death of perhaps 200,000 people and a Biafra-style famine, was effectively suppressed for over 4 years. Renewed attacks on the population are in progress now, and are also being suppressed.

I doubt that any story has ever received the coverage of the downing of KAL flight 007 last fall, sure proof that the Russians are the most barbaric devils since Attila the Hun so that we must place Pershing missiles in Germany and step up the war against Nicaragua. The densely-printed *NY Times* index devotes 7 full pages to the atrocity in September 1982 alone. In the midst of the furore, UNITA, the "freedom fighters" supported by the US and South Africa, took credit for downing an Angolan jet with 126 killed. There was no ambiguity, the plane was not off course flying over sensitive installations, there was no RC 135 US reconnaissance jet nearby confusing the issue (possibly jamming radar). It was simply premeditated murder. The incident received 100 words in the *NY Times* and no comment anywhere in the media.

This is not the only such case. In October 1976, a Cuban airliner was bombed by CIA-backed terrorists, killing 73 civilians. In 1973 Israel downed a civilian plane lost in a sandstorm over the Suez canal with 110 killed. There was no protest, only editorial comments about how "No useful purpose is served by an acrimonious debate over the assignment of blame" *(NY Times)*. Four days later, Prime Minister Golda Meir visited the US where she was troubled with no embarrassing questions and returned with new gifts of military aircraft. Contrary to recent falsehoods, Israel refused to pay compensation or to accept any responsibility; it offered only *ex gratia* payments, funded by the usual generous donor from abroad. In 1955, an Air India plane carrying the Chinese delegation to the Bandung conference was blown up in the air in what the Hong Kong police called a "carefully planned mass murder." An American defector later claimed that it was he who planted the bomb in the service of the CIA. None of these incidents demonstrate "barbarism"; all have been quickly forgotten.

One can offer thousands of such examples. In such ways, history is shaped in the interests of those in power.

All of this falls under the rubric of what Walter Lippmann, in 1921, called "the manufacture of consent," an art which is "capable of great refinements" and will lead to a "revolution" in "the practice of democracy." This art has been much admired in the social sciences. The well-known American political scientist Harold Lasswell wrote in 1933 that we must avoid "democratic dogmatisms," such as the belief that people are "the best judges of their own interests." Democracy permits the voice of the people to be heard, and it is the task of the intellectual to ensure that this voice endorses what far-sighted leaders know to be the right course. Propaganda is to democracy what violence is to totalitarianism. The techniques have been honed to a high art, far beyond anything that Orwell dreamt of. The device of feigned dissent, incorporating the doctrines of the state religion and eliminating rational critical discussion is one of the more subtle means, though simple lying and suppression of fact and other crude techniques are also highly effective.

It should be noted that ideological control (Agitprop) is far more important in the democracies than in states that rule by violence, and is therefore more refined, and more effective. There are no Danchevs here, except at the remote margins of political debate.

For those who stubbornly seek freedom, there can be no more urgent task than to come to understand the mechanisms and practices of indoctrination. These are easy to perceive in the totalitarian societies, much less so in the system of "brainwashing under freedom" to which we are subjected and which all too often we serve as willing or unwitting instruments.

Prisons — 1984 and After

by Claire Culhane

The role of prisons in capitalist society has a political function which is similar to that of the State, whose main interest is power and control. While the power of the military and the police within that context is readily understood by radical analysts, they have a tendency to avoid looking at prisons in the same way. Failing to make this link, the further tendency is to entirely omit any inclusion of prisons in the political analysis of such serious matters as nuclear war, racism, women, poverty, and so on.

This view, of course, stems from the attitude that prisons are filled with the dregs of society and we haven't the time to worry about them. In reality, we are dealing with the most political of social institutions and it is for *political* reasons that we should be paying more attention to the savagery, corruption and stupidity of the prison system, one of Canada's growth industries. The 1982-83 budgetary expenditure fund for the Solicitor-General's department, inclusive of the Royal Canadian Mounted Police (RCMP), the National Parole Board (NPB), the Correctional Service of Canada (CSC), and the Secretariat, was $1.3 billion, an 11.4% increase over the previous year.[1]

When *Amnesty International* exposes torture and murder of civilians in military dictatorships, it is readily accepted that these actions are political reprisals. When *Amnesty International* exposed torture of prisoners during the recent violent aftermath of a prison riot (such as in the Archambault Prison in Québec in 1982), it should also be viewed as brutality by guards — who represent State authority — against prisoners (reacting to prolonged, unwarranted physical and psychological abuse) who represent one of the most repressed sections of our society.

In the following discussion it will be argued that the *reasons* for incarceration are secondary to the *use* of incarceration as a political instrument. When a people become so accustomed to and accepting of naked force, which imprisonment represents, it is well on its way to condoning authoritarianism as a method to 'punish lawbreakers' and constitutes a mindless acceptance of State power, an acceptance which is not otherwise so easily tolerated.

The uncompromising power of the State through its so-called Criminal Justice System was best described by the late Chief Justice Bora Laskin when he characterized the National Parole Board (NPB) as "...a tyrannical authority... without precedent among administrative agencies empowered to deal with a person's liberty."[2] The NPB is accountable to no other body — not Parliament — not the Solicitor-General — nor the courts.

The pattern of institutionalized violence has become so commonplace that most people, even amongst prison activists and genuinely concerned lawyers, have reluctantly come to accept its seeming inevitability, and feel helpless to change. How to break through this wall of impotence, since we can no longer afford to accept that the same society which justifiably repudiates violence in its streets tolerates, at the same time, the various levels of violence practised against prisoners.

A thoroughgoing breakdown is needed to demonstrate how the system uses prisons to score its own points. We can no longer search out causes and solutions for rampant unemployment, racism and sexism without first recognizing that it is, for the most part, the *victims* of these practices who fill our prisons.

We need to understand that the prison system is an integral part of the growing drift towards the authoritarianism that is taking place in our alleged liberal democracy.

This tendency is also found in the alarming increase in the proliferation of weaponry. We live in an era where military budgets take precedence over all other social expenditures. "The USA currently has 30,000 nuclear weapons, 10,000 more than the Soviets, and it plans to build 17,000 more hydrogen bombs over the next ten years. We also know that Reagan plans to spend $2.5 trillion dollars on the military in the next five years... such enormous military expenditure (is) calculated to 'totally break the back of the USA economy'."[3]

There are frightening links between militarism and the penal system, as Helen Durie, a criminologist and feminist anti-militarist activist, in an unpublished article, most competently demonstrates:

"Just as nuclear weapons are used by the nuclear powers as the ultimate form of intimidation over those States which threaten their controlling interest over the world's resources and power, prisons similarly serve to maintain existing power and class relationships within every so-called developed society.

While the State's military forces prepare for organized and legalized violence on an international scale, prisons (along with the police) are the State's internal arm of systematic legalized violence. Their very presence and potential use is intimidating, and it doesn't require much analysis to see just who the reality, or the threat of imprisonment, is intended for.

It is important from the outset to make some distinction between the State's prison system, or police or military forces, and the individuals who serve in them, in describing them as purposeful violent institutions. It is probably fair to say that most men (and women too, in this age of 'equal rights') who are recruited into one of these services is not doing so in order to be able to kill, or even to use violence.

They are enticed by the financial benefits and promise of variety, adventure and education opportunities, and by the culturally-encouraged image of 'serving one's country'. That is how the State wants and needs it to be. It is not coincidental, either, of course, that those who do the front-line work — the real dirty work — in these professions are recruited predominantly from the lower socio-economic groups, where the lack of other educational, work and income opportunities make these enticements most salient and attractive. The fact that these people will be used by the State to carry out its wars against members of their own social groups at home and abroad is not part of their consciousness or service training... While there are many differences between military training, and the training received by police and prison guards there are also many similarities (such as regular inter-force shooting competitions), because all services must learn to automatically resort to violence under certain conditions.

Today we are witnessing a simultaneous build-up of military capability and threats, along with an expansion of the tools and use of internal repression. This is a result of the increasing material gap between the haves and have-nots, within societies and on an international level, even while the foundations of capitalism are disintegrating in the face of growing competition for depleting resources and cheap labour, and increasing international political consciousness...

It is not surprising, then, in this climate of increasing social unrest, that prisons are being used more, new prisons are being built, and the violent and repressive measures that operate inside prisons are being extended. In Canada, a few examples are the construction of additional Special Handling Units (super-maximum segregation), installation of more and more draconian security equipment, searching and electronic surveillance of visitors, and increased power to the Parole Board to indefinitely delay (justifiable) release. The rising suicide rate in prisons is just one attestation to the increasing physical and psychological brutality (and futility) of imprisonment.

In Canada, there are close to 250 'correctional facilities' with over 25,000 prisoners on any given day, at an annual cost of more than 1 billion, and increasing every year...

And who are these prisons for?

They are for those who learn only too well the meaning and power of 'success' in this society, and who dare to use the same tactics of intimidation, violence and lack of concern for others to achieve it as do the political and economic elite, but are without access to their legalized means... for those who can't afford the cost of legal protection... for those who dare to be poor and who refuse to live gratefully and passively on meagre handouts... for those who are born into a social — economic position which deprives them of the education and skills necessary to earn an 'honest' living and who dare to use other means to seek escape from their demeaning poverty... for Native people, whose dignified way of life has been stripped away by the white man and replaced with the dehumanizing and deadly life of alcohol... for women who refuse any longer to be subjected to routine beatings from a man and who dare to fight back... for women whose socialized and economic dependency on men, and their fear of them, draws them into criminal complicity... for those who, without the cover of domestic or legal protection, dare to act out the sexual violence towards women and children that is glorified in our culture every day... for those who refuse to learn to kill and be the cannon fodder for wars that are fought to protect the interests of the political and economic elite... for those whose political awareness dares them to challenge and defy the political and economic structures that provide the basis for nuclear weapons and all of the other essential, immoral and oppressive elements of militarism...

For the State, the connections (between militarism and prison) come easily, as can be seen, for example, in the frequent conversion of decommissioned military bases to prisons, or the regularly-touted proposal to sentence youthful offenders to a term in the military.

... Activists need also to be aware of how easily and readily prisons are used to suppress dissent and, in this increasingly ominous climate of inter-connectedness, recognize how integral a part of our political analysis the function of prisons must become."

The Canadian government is not unaware of the dangerous situation that presently exists in its penitentiaries. In 1977 Parliament heard from an all-party sub-committee that:

"A crisis exists in the Canadian Penitentiary System. It can be met only by the immediate implementation of large-scale reform... it is imperative that the Solicitor-General act immediately... as a matter of the utmost urgency."[4]

The Solicitor-General's response was to reject outright this first of 65 recommendations.

By 1984, with another four investigations (three International, and one by the Moderator of the United Church in Canada) the call for a full, public, impartial enquiry (as opposed to government-appointed) continues to escalate.

In any case, it is evident that far more than "large-scale reform" is needed to resolve the escalating turbulence of the prison system, as noted in the following paraphrase from an ecology manifesto:

"The disastrous pillage of the prison population must cease. The only way to stop it is to fight the material and social base which sustains it, that is, the system of capitalist production based on profit."

The crisis within our penitentiary system exists within, and is related to, the larger social context where crises presently exist in all aspects of social life, such as unemployment, health care, education, housing and growing poverty.

Radical movements, intent on dealing with these issues, are not only redefining their politics, but are also recognizing the necessity to build a mass movement that can effectively meet this crisis. It is within this context that prison activists must strive to build bridges with other groups. This is now beginning to happen.

"It is difficult to deny the momentum which has built up for an examination of the prison system. Public consciousness of prison issues and media interest in them has increased significantly."[5]

One of the most urgent issues that must be brought to public awareness is the criminal acts committed by the 'keepers' of prisoners:

"It should also be noted that many of the crimes committed by prisoners currently in New South Wales prisons pale into insignificance when compared with the systematic, calculated and brutal use and dereliction of public and legal duty of a large number of so-called responsible members of the community."[6]

Prisoners face a desperate battle just to survive the monstrous odds stacked against them, as 'criminals'. At last, society is slowly becoming aware of this situation. The more enlightened members of the Church, heeding their troubled consciences, are beginning to speak out. Bishop Remi De Roo had this to say to the Victoria Bar Association:

"The Canadian Criminal Justice System is vindictive and favors the rich over the poor... incarceration is a total failure as far as the churches are concerned... capital punishment and humiliating alternatives to incarceration are morally deplorable because they do not recognize the value and dignity of human life... society is not being protected by increasing the number of institutions holding increasing numbers of offenders, all of whom eventually return to society, angry and bitter."[7]

Canada jails more people than any other industrialized western country, except the USA. Canada's rate of incarceration is 150 persons out of every 100,000*. The USA's rate is 212. Other countries have a much lower incarceration rate, e.g. "for England and Wales it is 85, France 67, Sweden 65, Netherlands 28."[8]

With a 27% increase in the Federal prison population since 1980 — from 9,242 to 12,001 — Dennis Finlay, spokesperson for the Solicitor-General (sportswriter turned instant prison expert) still maintains the penitentiaries are "coping fairly well... we can't build overnight, and it takes six to seven years' lead time to build a major institution."[9] New institutions would thus have to be built every four months if they were to keep up with the dramatic increase in the prison population. Mr. Finlay offers the further insightful conclusion that since "...there are more prisoners coming in than going out... it puts a strain on resources."[10]

"The latest estimates quoted from the construction costs for Renous Maximum Security — Canada's Alcatraz — (formally named Atlantic Institution) ... deep in the woodlands of central New Brunswick, 108 miles north-east of Moncton... plan for $73 million... works out to $228,000 per cell or 30% more than any other Canadian institution... 'They're literally going to exile hundreds of prisoners... they're out of their minds by going against what every study on the location of prisons has recommended' charges Real Jubinville of the Canadian Association for the Prevention of Crime (CAPC) ..."[11]

Furthermore, Renous which will house the two highest security ratings in the one institution... (up to 240 Protective Custody and up to 80 Special Handling Unit

---

* Calculated from data Solicitor-General's Report 1982-83.

prisoners) is to be staffed by approximately 365 personnel. This will result in a high staff to prisoner ratio. Since prisoners are transferred at the absolute discretion of prison officials, how many more will be entombed in this formidable, far-away fortress to preserve the required ratio to keep those 365 staff fully employed?

And of course there are the further costs — staggering *human* costs — too devastating to contemplate, but contemplate we must!

"More than 27 prisoners a year are dying in Federal institutions mostly as a result of suicide or murder — 219 prisoners and staff had died in prisons in an 8 year period beginning Jan. 1/76..."[12]

Five homicides occurred in Kingston prisons within 13 weeks into 1984, and as many assaults again, while in 1983 alone there were 16 suicides, 65 attempted suicides, 276 self-mutilations, 389 assaults on prisoners, 121 assaults on staff, 7 prison murders and 1 staff murder, according to an editorial in a Kingston journal.[13]

Society must also recognize that one of the major reasons nothing is done to radically reform the penal system is because prisoners are an integral and necessary component of our economic structure. Prisoners provide a large pool of cheap labour for capitalist production, and do not pose the same problems for industry that a unionized work-force does. For example:

"Forty Correction industries staff who were attending a CSC National Industries Conference in Cornwall, Ont. visited Raybrook Federal Correctional Institution in Lake

Placid, N.Y. and were surprised to find that Raybrook's industrial operation pays for the costs of the total institution and also makes a profit... they were very impressed with its pay plan... it has two factories which manufacture gloves and printing products, and a third which is ready to open, which will produce pyjamas, sheets, pillow cases, etc... inmates are paid 44 cents to $1.05 per hour... with no pay for any absences from work, and pay is dependent upon satisfactory conduct and production. The aim... is to produce a quality product, deliver it on time, cover all expenses and make a profit."[14]

The following issue of *LET'S TALK* announced CSC's own progress, through CORCAN**, whose major objective this year:

"...is to increase its contribution to overhead through the production of industrial goods in the most cost effective way... also very important is the development of good work habits to inmates as well as giving them the chance to learn marketable skills (sic)... some problems: most of goods sold and cost of materials, selling and distribution were too high..."[15]

And in Bowden, Alberta, we find that prisoners are employed in the production of "furniture, upholstery,

** Revenue generated through the sales of CORCAN manufactured products... amounted to $10,308,000 during 1982-83, a 38% increase over 1981-82; value of agricultural products produced during 1982-83 was $1,280,000: an increase of 28.5% over 1981-82.
   CSC is restricted to selling goods and services... to Federal, provincial and municipal governments and to charitable, religious or non-profit organisations unless (sic) special authorization is obtained from Treasury Board.[16]

83

carpentry, metal products and the Drone Rocket Project... part of an innovative... modification of a number of discontinued American-made drone rockets to be used for target practice by the Canadian Navy... involving the Canadian Armed Forces at Suffield, Alberta." (emphasis added).[17]

As 'privatization' (the reduction of government services by placing them in the hands of private industry which must find ways to operate at a profit) reaches out to hospitals, child care, legal aid and halfway houses, it should come as no surprise that a similar move is taking place in the penitentiary system.

Prisons also provide employment, especially for professionals. In an address to the Canadian Psychologists Association, So.-Gen. Kaplan urged them "...to join us in the efforts to make things better... our Federal penitentiary system now employs approximately 70 psychologists and we wish we had more."[18] There seems to be no end to the lush Criminal Justice pasture of vested interests beckoning every profession, trade and careerist.

Half a century ago, George Bernard Shaw described prisons as perpetuating an expensive, futile and self-defeating system, and it is still true. Today our economy may be in a shambles, but our prison system continues to be a major growth industry used first, last and always as an instrument of control.

Although all the stated goals of prisons have yet to be met, they continue to operate as the product of the political economy of capitalist development. In addition to activists, idealists, 'left' realists, and reformists who are calling for immediate practical action, there are also some establishment figures who, when referring to prison policies, express themselves in what might almost be described as 'class conscious revolutionary' terms.

One might reasonably conclude that a growing number of people from all walks of life recognize that regardless of the political and economic advantages or disadvantages presented, imprisonment has failed miserably as a means of reducing crime. Such declarations have become a device to gain credibility and audience with the public and policy-makers alike. Even though the biased functioning of the Courts and law enforcement structures *do* win convictions for most of the highly publicized and sensationalist crimes, were we to succeed in changing the prison system, the question of what to do with lawbreakers would obviously still have to be addressed.

Decarceration — phasing out the vast majority who do not require institutionalization — has been put forward by serious students as a way of relieving intolerable overcrowding, to name only one of the burgeoning evils. They believe that about 80% of prisoners, neither violent nor dangerous to the community nor to themselves, could conceivably be placed in a community-supervised employment where they could continue to support themselves and their families, pay taxes, make restitution to their victim(s) and of even more practical value — reduce the huges cost of maintaining the prison system. Even the Commissioner of Corrections conceded in 1979 that "40% of those in prison are in for other than violent crimes".[19] Assuming that they do not need to be locked up, by 1984's count of almost 12,000, that would mean approximately 4,800 should have been released by now, or never imprisoned in the first place. Obviously this is not happening.

However, how realistic is this proposal? In a country with close to two million unemployed, would these ex-prisoners be able to find work? To make matters worse, the Solicitor-General "expects to have more than 1000... serving the minimum 25 years before parole eligibility" by the year 2,000.[20] Such eligibility by no means guarantees that they will ever be released.

One has to wonder if by detaining so many for so long is another method of holding them hostage to the present bankrupt economy, as was clearly the case during the 19th century Industrial Revolution? During that period, as we know, the landowners labelled the dispossessed rural people as vagrants and had them thrown into work houses, also known as prisons.

Since prisons and the capitalist economy are so deeply interdependent, should we attempt to alter the prison system without transcending capitalist relations of production. We can see how decarceration would only serve to bring about further unemployment, social strains, and inevitably more recidivism. But it is precisely because of these abhorrent, degrading conditions coupled with the criminal treatment inflicted upon prisoners, that the dismantling of the prison system must remain a major focus of political analysis.

Displaying considerable insight into this problem, the Coalition for Prisoners Rights Newsletter challenges the philosophy that "...longer sentences or death penalties are the ultimate solution to the problem of crime. The real problems of our prison system go ignored. Society has not dealt with:

1) "the unequal distribution of this country's wealth;
2) the use of our legal and judicial system to punish those who are poor;
3) the failure to deal with drug abuse syndrome;
4) the failure to provide the jobs needed by people to survive and feed and take care of their families without having to commit crimes to do so."[21]

The Criminal Justice System continues to extend its control beyond prison walls. Space does not permit a more detailed description of the net-widening structures closely supervised by the parole system, such as alternative (halfway houses) and diversion programmes (probation). However, there are also surveillance programmes calculated to undermine the very concept of the abolition of the prison system.

In what would appear to be staunch support for the prison abolition theory, Professor Ezzat Fattah, Chairperson of the Criminology Dept. at Simon Fraser University (and one of the original Citizens Advisory Committee members at the B.C. Penitentiary in 1976) while outlining possible alternatives to incarceration "...suggests abolition of prisons [as a strategy] to persuade society to accept alternatives such as 'incapacitation without incarceration." He then proceeds to present examples, such as "confiscation of firearms or drivers' licences when unlawfully used; separation of wife-beaters from spouses, and removal of children from abusive parents." However, although the professor does sound a note of caution that "...electronic devices to monitor an offenders' movements are open to abuse and would require legal safeguards", he goes on to add that "they could be useful to ensure that he (sic) remains within court-ordered boundaries."[22] Prof. Fattah's concern about legal abuses however does not really include concern for the rights of prisoners. In the USA electronic attachments are already being used:

"...a small radio transmitter attached to a plastic band and worn as an anklet emits a signal that is picked up by a receiver attached to the probationer's telephone...in turn relays the signal to a computer... if the departures listed on the computer printout don't match the probationer's work curfews, then probation officers go to check on their client."[23]

Faced with the absence of rule of law inside prisons, it can be expected that many prisoners, deeply resentful of this lack, will opt for this form of 'house arrest' at the earliest opportunity. Another feature of this 'incapacitation without incarceration' scenario may be found in proposed penal colonies, already dubbed

'Limited Access Correctional Communities' (LACC). As well as for long-term offenders and their families, they will also provide — let us be warned — a convenient facility to exile others to, who will be seen to constitute a 'threat to national security' — demonstrators against nuclear installations, ecological destruction, and so on. This places still another weapon in the hands of this (or any other) government, to be used against alleged dangerous war resisters.

All these high-powered schemes to protect the community from dangerous criminals must be seen also as dangerous controls which can be used to reinforce political solutions to economic problems when the time comes for the State to silence workers' and protestors in so many other sectors.

The problem with this kind of high tech(nology) research is that it could lead to even more electronic surveillance, ignoring the human element altogether. One would have to measure this approach against the one advanced by William Kunstler, the prominent American Civil Rights lawyer, at the 112th Congress of Corrections in Ontario.

"I have been led to believe during all my adult life, that there are human answers for human problems and that there is an obligation upon all of us to seek those answers in an intelligent and determined way. Reason, Descartes tells us, is the highest attibute of humankind, the quality that supposedly sets us apart from other animals... the creation of such an outlaw prison class will, in the long run, jeopardize and perhaps destroy the freedoms of us all as well as advance the dehumanization process that constantly gnaws at the fabric of our vaunted civilization."[24]

Following the most gruesome riot in Canadian prison history which erupted in July 1982 at the Archambault Maximum Security Prison just north of Montreal, in which three guards were killed and two prisoners committed suicide, there was an unanimous call for an independent investigation from, amongst others *Amnesty International* which noted that "...the Canadian government has an international obligation to undertake a full, independent and impartial investigation." This has not been carried out — as yet.

Since this essay has been started, (in early 1984) Millhaven Maximum Security and Collins Bay Medium Security, both in the Kingston, Ontario area, have been the scene of five murders, six assaults, continuous lock-ups, army manoeuvers around the prison perimeter and prisoners handcuffed during yard recreation period — in a four month period — eliciting the expression of concern from a Crown Prosecutor, Jack McKenna that the Federal penitentiaries in that area "...appear to be totally out of control," re-emphasizing his own observations made more than five years earlier about the "degradation and torture which some... prisoners must suffer... we should by this time be looking for a new approach to the problem."[25]

This has proven to be a mere prelude to the further tragic deaths of two more guards at Stony Mountain Medium Security Prison in Winnipeg, Manitoba, built for no more than 400 but now with 100 prisoners too many — another chapter to the same prison "which has had a series of tense incidents in recent years including murder of a prison official in the seventies — in August 1982, prisoners went on a rampage at the jail to protest double-bunking."[26] The tragedy is compounded by the Commissioner's concept of a solution as reported in the same journal "...trying to alleviate problems... by transferring some prisoners temporarily to other institutions."[27]

The proposal to the Millhaven administration for an immediate meeting between administration, prisoners and some outside reputable observers to serve as liaison and to make the prisoners' position known to the public (instead of the usual mainly official version) has yet to be considered. Instead, a voluminous (May 1984) *Report Of The Study Group On Murders And Assaults In The Ontario Region* has been produced, following the well-worn pattern of all previous government studies. It spaces itself from the reality of the prisoners' dilemma, and produces no concise, workable solutions. For example, when reference is made to the fact that "Centralization came about as a result of the demand for the rule of law in Canadian prisons and the need for fiscal restraints,"[28] the impression is left that these two demands were met. The rule of law has yet to be established!!

And when they conclude (in Recommendation 18, p. 112) that "...we do not think that our society will tolerate human 'warehousing', again they are flying in the face of grim reality. The numbing boredom resulting from lack of work and/or programmes, the hopelessness and bitterness aggravated by excessively long sentences — makes a farce of the cynical declaration that they "...do not believe... that an inmate should be left to his (sic) own devices or that his (sic) survival should be left to chance".

The difficulty in finding some useful solutions to the critical prison problems is not unlike the complexity which face us as we search for solutions to the many contradictions of the capitalist system itself. The situation is exacerbated by the fact that prisoners possess the least power to enable them to organize any significant resistance, mainly due to the severe restrictions and corruption in their community. What is required then is that grassroots organizations work to expose and educate and build resistance to the erosion of civil and human rights in the prison system.

It therefore becomes all the more incumbent upon those of us *outside* in the free (!) world to ensure that the rule of law is respected inside prisons. We should not lose sight of the fact that those same prisons have been historically used to incarcerate other types, as political events dictate. We need only examine a few of the observations addressed to the prison scene by the Paris-based International Federation of Human Rights (following their 1983 investigation into the aftermath of the Archambault Riot) to more fully appreciate how fragile is the state of affairs vis-à-vis human rights in our society when our prisons have yet to maintain a basic level of security for its occupants:

1. "The principle of the rule of law must prevail inside Canadian prisons.

2. The Correctional Investigator must be responsible to Parliement and not to the Solicitor-General.

3. The penitentiary system must be operated openly and be subject to the control of the citizenry.

4. Canada must immediately cease its violations of international agreements (Universal Declaration of Human Rights, International Covenant of Civil and Political Rights, and the Standard Minimum Rules for the Treatment of Prisoners — adopted by Canada, August 1975);

5. Canada must be considered to have shown contempt for human dignity and to have denied the objectives of the United Nations Charter;

6. Canada must be considered guilty of violations of basic human rights and freedoms;

7. The International Federation of Human Rights must do all in its power to put an end to this situation and keep the United Nations informed in this matter."[29]

However, "keeping the United Nations informed" would have to include reference to other matters where the Canadian government continues to ignore its commitments — for example, amendments to the Parole Act passed by Parliament in 1977 provided that when a Federal prisoner's parole is revoked, the time spent outside prison on parole must be counted as time served. The Solicitor-General has made it clear that even if the U.N. finds that Canada is violating the Covenant, the government won't consider itself bound by the finding "because we are a sovereign state", as he constantly reminds himself.

The same attitude prevails when called to account for violations under the Canadian Charter of Rights which guarantees the right to vote to every Canadian citizen. Once again, the Solicitor-General denies prisoners their rights, secure in the knowledge that there are no provisions for the United Nations to force any member-nation to abide by its recommendations.

When he submitted his John Howard Society of Alberta's supportive brief for the granting of voting rights to prisoners, Daniel Howe, its Executive Director, felt that "...people who hold a Neanderthal mentality toward the treatment of prisoners must realize that when they [the prisoners] are released, their actions will reflect values they've adopted in prison."[30]

Closer to home for most of us are the government edicts which serve to restrain *all* Canadians, not just prisoners. Note should be taken of Order-in-Council PC. 1981-1305 which assigns special powers to the Solicitor-General under the newly created Emergency Powers Order (EPO):

"No. 6 To establish, administer and operate civilian internment camps;
No. 7 To facilitate the selective reduction and transfer of prison population to provide for the establishment of civilian internment camps."

In reply to our written request for an explanation of Clause No. 7, the *Prisoners' Rights Group* was advised in a personal communication dated May 10/82 from the office of the Sol-Gen:

"... no subsequent document has been issued that negates Sections 6 & 7 of the Order; with further reference to No. 6, since PC 1981-1305 is a planning order only, it provides no implementation authority. This means that no facilities may be constructed in advance of an actual war. I would like also to note that so far this matter has a low priority and I have not yet seen any option from my officials and none are yet in preparation."

We are no further enlightened by this response except to have our worst fears confirmed, namely that this measure was primarily aimed at striking a balance between the government's version of the rights of the individual and national security.

It took only little over a year to introduce the next measure — Bill C-9, which established the Canadian Security Intelligence Service (CSIS). This has been described (by Alan Borovoy, Legal Counsel for the Canadian Civil Liberties Association) as a mechanism:

"...whereby citizens may have their conversations bugged, mail opened, homes searched and tax files invaded... a mandate to use such intrusive surveillance for the monitoring of 'activities... in support of... acts of violence... for the purpose of achieving a political objective within Canada or a foreign state...' this bill must be seen as a threat to law-abiding people and legitimate dissent."[31]

Ironically, a similar mandate has existed in the prison system for decades. When we are assured that this Bill C-9 will permit security operatives to break the law when it is 'reasonably necessary to enable them to perform', we find a chilling parallel to the account of the brutalities carried out on prisoners in the wake of the Archambault riot, events which the same Solicitor-General still refuses to acknowledge. What basis is there for us to anticipate any different reaction from the same government officials when they begin to impose similar measures on *citizens* as they have on *prisoners* over the years?

When the incarcerated, who represent the most vulnerable section of society in terms of lack of opportunity to defend themselves against the variety of physical and psychological abuses, can be, and are, beaten and gassed with impunity, we face the grave risk of seeing the same methods extend to other layers of society, until and unless a sufficiently united effort succeeds in stemming the tide of the earlier repressions.

The prison system, by consequence, is tradionally used as a convenient testing ground. There is a stark relevance to Pastor Niemoller's classic statement about "remaining silent when the Nazis came for the Communists... the Jews... the Protestants... by that time there was no one left to speak for me." As long as so many remain silent when prisoners are abused, there will be that many fewer left to speak up when non-prisoners are equally abused by the same forces.

In the same connection, the Nuremberg War Crime Tribunal spelled out the individual's responsibility when faced with orders received from superiors. As stated in another context relating to the preservation of the environment:

"...anyone who is aware that crimes of the state are being committed has an obligation to take what action they can to prevent that from occurring."[32]

Since, generally speaking, too many people still remain relatively poorly informed on the true nature of the prison system** it becomes increasingly evident that in order to formulate any meaningful political analysis, it must include the essential role that prisons play in reinforcing the controls which the State requires to remain in power.

It is also evident that the Canadian Justice system has a tendency to respond to 'street' crime by increasing its overall controls.

Positioning the prison system within the capitalist system, paralleling all its contradictions, injustices, deprivations and horrors, it can be more clearly understood that until we accept the reality that imprisonment is one of the ways in which the State deals with our poor, our women and children, our minority groups and our unemployed, we will not be able to respond realistically to the disturbing functions of the prison system.

Armed with this understanding, a more comprehensive analysis can be made of the various economic, political and social measures which the State uses to preserve its power.

Identifying the struggle to abolish the prison system (appropriately described as a 'bottomless pit') with the struggle to abolish war, poverty and injustice for all, would also constitute an innovative change in the prevailing attitude towards prisoners — 95% of whom come from the economically and socially deprived class. This would add a measure of compassion towards this otherwise neglected section of human beings with whom we share our world. Not to be overlooked is the enriching experience for all concerned.

Although Canadian prisoners cannot be considered political prisoners in the same sense as are prisoners in countries fighting for their liberation against foreign powers or repressive national governments, it is the struggle to dismantle the power structure inherent in the prison system, and the structures which must be dealt with in the universal struggle for freedom and independence, which remains basic to this analysis.

** A Gallup Poll in which Canadians were asked: In your opinion, of every 100 crimes committed in Canada, what percentage involve violence, for example, where the victim was beaten up, raped, robbed at gunpoint and so on? Respondents estimated 53.9%. In fact the number of crimes of violence in the past few years in Canada has amounted to no more than 8% of all offences reported to police.[33]

The intention of this essay is to link the prison abolition movement with all other political struggles for fundamental change — a formidable task, but one which must be tackled with a passion.

NOTES

[1] Solicitor-General Annual Report, 1982-83, p. 17.
[2] Mitchell vs. the Queen, 24 CCC 2D 245, Supreme Court of Canada.
[3] "Putting an End to Nuclear Madness", Dr. Helen Caldicott, *Briarpatch,* April, 1984, p. 7-8.
[4] *Report to Parliament* by the Sub-Committee on the Penitentiary System in Canada, 2nd Session of the Thirtieth Parliament, 1976-77, p. 2.
[5] Zdenkowski, G. and Brown, D. *The Prison Struggle: Changing Australia's Penal System,* Penguin Books, 1982, p. 190.
[6] Ibid., p. 165.
[7] *Times-Colonist,* Victoria, Apr. 13, 1984.
[8] Council of Europe, *Prison Information Bulletin,* No. 2, December 1983.
[9] *Globe and Mail,* Toronto, July 18, 1984.
[10] Ibid.
[11] *Toronto Star,* Toronto, July 3, 1984.
[12] *Globe and Mail,* Toronto, May 11, 1984.
[13] *Whig Standard,* Kingston, Mar. 31, 1984.
[14] *Let's Talk,* Ottawa, Dec. 15, 1983.
[15] *Let's Talk,* Jan. 15, 1984.
[16] Solicitor-General Annual Report, 1982-83, p. 66-67.
[17] *Let's Talk,* March 15, 1984.
[18] *Liaison,* Sept. 1983.
[19] *Ottawa Citizen,* March 10, 1979,
[20] *Let's Talk,* October 15, 1983.
[21] Coalition for Prisoners' Rights Newsletter, Santa Fe, New Mexico, Vol. 9, No. 2, March 1984.
[22] *Liaison,* Feb. 1983.
[23] *Let's Talk,* May 15, 1983.
[24] *Jericho,* National Moratorium on Prison Construction Newsletter, Washington, D.C. No. 30, Winter 1982.
[25] *Whig Standard,* Jan. 31, 1984.
[26] *SUN,* Vancouver, July 15, 1984.

[27] Ibid., July 19, 1984.
[28] *Report Of The Study Group On Murders And Assaults In The Ontario Region,* May 18, 1984, p. 80.
[28] *Rapport de Mission sur la Situation au Pénitencier Archambault,* France, Dec. 16, 1982, p. 75.
[30] *Edmonton Journal,* May 17, 1984.
[31] *Globe and Mail,* May 26, 1983.
[32] Richard Falk, *Ground Zero* July/Aug. 1983.
[33] Royal Bank Letter, *Punishment and Crime,* Vol. 65, No. 3, May-June 1984.

Towards New Forms of Resistance

by Yolande Cohen

It is awkward for a historian like myself to speak of "new" forms of resistance when by all appearances the relentlessness with which human beings resist in order to subsist has endured since time immemorial. This is a constant factor which I would not presume to challenge. My present intention, however, is to touch upon the particular aspect assumed by the resistance of individuals in regard not only to the encroachments of power upon themselves, but also in regard to the resistance which arises from their relationship to power itself. I am not about to undertake here a history of the revolts or revolutions which have marked the passage of this century, and which bear witness to opposition, or to occasional conflicts with established powers. I shall attempt, rather, to elicit some of the feelings which inspired them — and I deliberately choose the term feeling rather than struggle or combat, which belong to a political vocabulary which is often borrowed from the military. So I offer some random thoughts inspired by many years of research into Western history of the 20th century, observed through the spyglass of the history of human rights and rights of the citizen, recently renamed rights of the person. I propose a schematic outline in order to characterize each of three stages by those uncertain feelings which may be called 1) egalitarian utopia, 2) submission to force, 3) liberatory love. For each stage there corresponds an imagined form of political power, 1) power with, 2) power over, 3) powerlessness.

I. Utopia corresponds to that great tidal wave, which one can trace back to the French Revolution, but which was already inspired by men such as Hume, Locke or Rousseau, and which consists of changing the rules of communal life. The basic principle of this major transformation was the desire to raise man to the level of humanity by allotting him a series of noble tasks, all the while promoting liberty and equality. Homogenizing industry permitted an egalitarian utopia to be partially realized, or at least allowed a potential of its realization to be glimpsed. Let us recall Orwell's words:

"And, in fact, without being used for any such purpose, but by a sort of automatic process — by producing wealth which it was sometimes impossible not to distribute — the machine did raise the living standards of the average human being very greatly over a period of about fifty years at the end of the nineteenth and the beginning of the twentieth centuries. But it was also clear that an all round increase in wealth threatened the destruction — of a hierearchical society."*

And the old hierarchical society reacts all the more strongly when the source of its order is threatened with extinction.

It is interesting to note that it is at the moment when the utopian character of equality becomes blurred that the project is most controversial. At the turn of the century in Europe one could see developing those strenuous confrontations between revolutionaries on both sides: on the one hand there were the advocates of an egalitarian society who organized those numer-

---

* *1984* by George Orwell, Penguin Books, 1954, p. 154-55.

ous leagues, associations, unions and parties, who wanted not only reform of civil rights with legal equality for all but also recognition of the individual, a totally separate person protected by the ancient *habeas corpus,* and over whom the State would henceforth be responsible.

It was no small task attempting to sort out these numerous claims from the elementary, yet overlooked principle of humanity towards all persons. In order to buttress the Charter of the Rights of Man they had recourse to the old principles of immutable individual rights, because they were natural. The League of the Rights of Man became their principal and inveterate defender. Social and socialist ideologies are also derived from them. Attempts were under way to invent the individual and his inalienable rights. Yet at the same time on the other hand there emerged that other tendency, no less active and claiming to be every bit as revolutionary, which proclaimed the individual to be part of a human group, that compact mass of individuals united in a common collective destiny. The accent is placed not upon the individual, but upon the group which is formed with others. An illuminating piece by Vacher de la Pouge explains the meaning of this belated and prophetic rehabilitation of the masses. (The Aryan, his social role 1889-90, Paris 1899, p. 512). (L'Aryen, son rôle social 1889-90, Paris 1899, p. 512).

"Every man is related to all men and to all living creatures. There are, therefore, no more rights of man than there are rights of three-banded armadillos, no more rights for web-fingered gibbons than for horses which are harnessed or for steers which are eaten. Man having lost the privilege of being apart, in the image of God, has no more rights than any other mammal. The very idea of rights is a fiction. There are only forces. Rights are pure conventions, transactions between equal or unequal powers; as soon as one of them ceases to be strong enough to make

the other recognize the validity of the transaction the right ceases.
Between members of a society a right is something which is sanctioned by collective strength. Between nations this guarantee of stability is absent. There is no right against force, for a right is no more than what the State creates by force, and latently maintains by it. All men are brothers, all animals are brothers, but being brothers is not enough to stop us from eating each other.
Long live fraternity, but woe to the losers! Life is only sustained by death. In order to live one must eat, and kill to eat."

This long quotation has the merit of being clear. Vacher de la Pouge was neither alone in his opinion nor isolated in his belief. Gustave de Bon, Tarde and many others developed this idea of the force of the masses. Equality would therefore lead to despotism of the masses. Tocqueville foretold it. I refer you to the work of Moscovici, *L'Age des Foules* (Tayard, 1983) for fuller descriptions and insightful analyses of this phenomenon.

II. The negation of the individual and of human rights, and the manipulation of the masses by the elite or by totalitarian States usher in an era of submission. Thinking that they are protected from slavery, that scourge, that absolute evil, by rights, the people undergo supreme penance; constrained to survive, they submit to the power of the strongest. The crazed power of Big Brother swoops down upon individuals and deprives them of their elementary protective reactions. Orwell elaborates at length upon this theme in the third part of his work. The Party wants the total annihilation of all normal human faculties in order to achieve the full exercise of its power. The sole objective is the pursuit of power for its own sake (p. 371) and for what it confers. Yet in more than one respect reality surpasses fiction. Some years after Orwell finished *1984* numerous works, pieces of evidence, and documents appeared, which let us catch a glimpse of the enormity of the totalitarian drama. From this abundance of writing, coming for the most part from Eastern Europe, I only wish to single out one, which was recently published in French by V. Grossman, entitled *Vie et Destin*. A vast family epic, it describes in human terms the inhumanity of the period of the Battle of Stalingrad.

Careful neither to judge, nor even to lament, Grossman makes us understand how men and women found themselves bound and tied. And that's the great perversion which the 20th century has accomplished (Grossman, p. 198):

> "In putting itself at the service of fascism, the soul of man proclaims that slavery, that absolute evil, bearer of misfortune and death, as the one and only object.
> Man does not renounce human feelings, but he proclaims that the crimes committed by fascism are a superior form of humanism; he agrees to divide people into the categories of pure and impure, worthy and unworthy.
> The will to survive at any price has resulted in the compromise of the soul with instinct."*

Emphasizing the hypnotic power of violence in the hands of the totalitarian State, Grossman like Orwell wonders if it will succeed in transforming human nature so as to wipe out the aspiration towards liberty (p. 199). In contrast to Orwell, Grossman remains preeminently optimistic and brings forth from the guts of man that force, that instinct for freedom, which alone involves condemnation of the totalitarian State. He is thus led to draw a distinction: "Man, condemned to slavery is a slave by destiny and not by nature. The aspiration of human nature towards liberty is invincible; it can be crushed but it cannot be annihi-

---

* Ed. Julliard, *L'Age d'Homme*, 1984.

lated" (p. 200). Grossman still objects to Big Brother. He will never like him, because for him 2 and 2 still makes 4 and all men still want to be free. He, who has lived through Stalingrad, continues to believe in freedom as the driving force of human beings. Their submission was the result of a contingency, when the devastating power of certain people prevailed. Against power no more equality which comes to terms with it, but liberty which emancipates from it.

The example of the Swedish diplomat Raoul Wallenberg, who managed with false papers to rescue almost 100,000 Jewish prisoners from Nazi Germany, is significant in this respect. He refused to go along with the lies of the fine society to which he belonged and bore witness to his ideals of humanity. He has apparently been rotting for almost 40 years in a Soviet prison, without anyone really being able to know whether he is alive or dead.

Thus some reasons for hope reach us in bits and pieces, without enabling us to give a full account of them. The post second world war period has been teeming with currents of ideas, but also with movements and actions in favour of this, in defence of that, etc... the human being is once again at the centre; one's liberty the most precious amongst one's goods.

III. In this last quarter of a century it would be an exaggeration to say that all has been rosy, that human beings have won back their freedom.

The mere existence of an organization like Amnesty International attests to the precariousness of the conditions in which it is exercised.

Since, however, I should like to finish on an optimistic note, perhaps one can see in these numerous examples of resistance by individuals to encroachment from many different powers certain reassuring signs. Moreover, and it is in this sense that I continue to harbour some hope, one can read into the protest movements of the sixties and seventies a certain turnaround of the process. In contrast to its predecessors the generation of the sixties and seventies did not rise up to claim its share of power, but rather to reject outright political power and its coercive force (the police), as well as its subtle daily influence (the consumer society). It was thus not a question of replacing one power by another, but rather of nullifying the strength of established power; by creating alongside, and not even in opposition, a network of individuals endowed with instinct, reason and perhaps imagination.

Love was their bond, and since they preferred to make love rather than war, this feeling became a liberating power. All individuals were not only equal — that was not the main concern — but they were free to be whatever they were: black, white, women, men, young, old, etc...

From elementary and passive resistance this force became a network, a movement of emancipation. The women's movement established itself in many respects as the way-station and then the bearer of these aspirations. It is no coincidence if the essential part of its impact derives from its capacity to make a private person into a totally separate entity. Without wanting to idealize a movement which experiences the vicissitudes of daily life and practice like any other, one should note here how much this articulation of the private element in politics opens up the perspective on a redefinition of power — and of the stance which women take in relationship to the powers that be.

Thus individuals, whoever they may be, one might say, are human entities capable as such of being the grain of sand which clogs the wheels. On condition, however, that they remember how hard they must struggle to remain human.

Translated by Robert Mayo

The Totality of Totalitarianism: Reflections and Perspectives

by Jean-Pierre Deslauriers

In a literary outburst which was typical for him, Proudhon once described the situation of the citizen who succumbs to the State: "To be governed, is to be, at every operation, at every transaction, with every movement, noted, registered, counted, given a fixed rate, stamped, measured, assessed, licensed, certified, authorized, given tentative approval, reprimanded, impeded, discharged, set straight, corrected. It is, under the pretext of public purposes, and in the name of the general interest, to be placed under requisition, made use of, held to ransom, exploited, subjected to monopolies, exposed to extortion, squeezed, baffled, robbed; then, at the least resistance, at the first word of complaint, suppressed, fined, vilified, harassed, hunted down, bullied, bludgeoned, disarmed, garrotted, imprisoned, shot, machine-gunned, judged, sentenced, transported, sacrificed, sold, betrayed, and to crown it all, mocked, ridiculed, insulted, dishonoured. That's government, that's its justice, that's its morality!"

This tirade could make one smile: obviously, Proudhon once again got carried away and let himself go in order to preach an overdose at his parishioners: how can one hold to such a definition of the State when one can see the progress of democratic societies, the development of workers' organizations, the raising of the level of schooling of the masses, the diffusion of information? No really, the author has gone a bit too far here! And in fact, more than one socialist has entertained hopes of using the State to change society; historically, quite a few have permitted themselves to be bewitched by its siren song, but without having the craftiness or the prudence of Ulysses. The warning from Proudhon and the anarchist movement was not heeded, and the socialist movement strayed on a Statist tangent. By concentrating powers in the State, the supposedly revolutionary movement gave birth to a form of government even more cruel than any which had been known. Proudhon's hyperbole was thus not only confirmed by the facts, but even surpassed by the course of events, to such an extent that our epoch designated this new kind of government as totalitarian.

"What does the totalitarian phenomenon consist of? This phenomenon, like all social phenomena, lends itself to multiple definitions, according to the aspect which the observer grabs onto. It seems to be that the five main elements are the following:

1. The totalitarian phenomenon occurs in a regime which grants one party a monopoly on political activity.

2. The monopolistic party is inspired by or fortified with an ideology upon which it confers absolute authority and which, consequently, becomes the official truth of the State.

3. In order to disseminate this official truth, the State in turn reserves unto itself a double monopoly, the monopoly over the means of force and another over the means of persuasion. All of the media, radio, television, and press are directed, controlled, by the State and those who represent it.

4. Most of the economic and professional activities are subservient to the State and become, in some way, part

of the State itself. Since the State is inseparable from its ideology, most economic and professional activities are tinged by the official truth.

5. Everything being henceforward a State activity, and all activities being subject to its ideology, an error committed in an economic or a professional activity is at the same time an ideological error. Thus one ends up with a politicization, an ideological transfiguration of all the possible errors which individuals may make, and, finally, with a form of terror which is both inquisitorial and ideological."
(Aron, 1965 : 287-8)

The main characteristic of totalitarianism consists, therefore, of the absorption of all social functions by the State itself, with the disappearance of civil society into Statist politics. In his subsequently famous novel, *1984,* George Orwell described the mechanism of this type of State. Just as with the description by Proudhon, the Orwellian depiction appeared rather loaded, perhaps even exaggerated, in the eyes of his contemporaries. Nevertheless, with time it has proved itself to be extremely pertinent.

One of the most powerful means at the disposal of any State, but which plays a primary role in the establishment of a totalitarian regime, is that of education. In the Eurasia of *1984* it focuses upon the acquisition of three mental processes: "crimethink", "blackwhite" and "doublethink". The first process designates the faculty of stopping short on the threshold of a dangerous thought. It includes the power of not grasping analogies, of not perceiving errors of logic, and of not understanding the simplest arguments if they stray beyond established norms. "Blackwhite" has several meanings: it signifies that black is white when the situation applies to the authorities, but that white is always black in reference to an opponent. As for "doublethink", it conveys the necessity of maintaining the infallibility of the established order by reinterpreting the past, even though it may entail contradictions. History is therefore continually re-examined in the light of changes of doctrine, of political line, of alliances, and of politicians. Through doublethink one ends up believing that these changes are real and that it has always been thus.

However far-fetched they may seem to be, these processes can be found in the actual behaviour of individuals. The classic consumer, on the one hand, attributes great importance to the ownership of goods: advertising provides him/her with a daily, weekly, monthly and annual ration of information about the new articles which s/he must acquire in order to achieve happiness. On the other hand, since s/he does not have the financial means to obtain these things, s/he renounces them *de facto* only to live through dreams and to sublimate fantasies. The same cannot be said for the delinquent, who not only clings to the dream, but attempts to realize it by all possible means, legal or not. As a member of that set pointed out to me: "There are no thieves in society: there are only capitalists!" If the delinquent appears to be deviant, it is not because s/he diverges from social norms, but rather because s/he tries to conform to them too strictly: s/he hasn't understood that "crimethink" is based upon an element of trickery and bad faith.

The crimethink developed by the educational system seeks to develop submission. In a famous experiment Stanley Milgram (1974) demonstrated how it is manifested in the actual behaviour of the ordinary citizen. In the course of an apparently scientific experiment, the author asked naive subjects to administer electric shocks under the pretext that they formed an integral part of a learning method. In general, 65% of the individuals complied and agreed to give shocks going as high as 450 volts. The researcher presumed that the prestige of the university could be a factor and took his experiment beyond the walls of academe, but the results remained the same.

How can one explain such conduct on the part of people living in a democratic regime? How can one explain such cruelty? In fact, the most sensible subjects were those who quit the experiment, but they were few in number. As Hampden-Turner rightly emphasizes (1973: 113-146), the most human ones were marginal figures. Milgram explains the results in the following manner. First of all, he distinguishes the autonomous state, i.e. one where the person considers her/himself to be responsible for his/her actions, from the agential state, where s/he defines him/herself in such a way that s/he accepts the total control of a person possessing a higher social status. In the latter case, s/he considers him/herself as a simple instrument destined to carry out the wishes of someone else. Military people and torturers share the frankness of Eichmann.

Milgram's explanation is more descriptive than analytical, but how can one not see the central role of the State which looms up behind the presumably individual deviations. One needs to remind oneself that the individual is first and above all a social product. In choosing between a citizen who behaves freely and another who demonstrates obedience, it goes without saying that the State prefers the second type: obedience within the family, at school, at work, in the hospital, in the army. Obedience, obedience, obedience: thus certain Soviet psychiatrists manage to interpret justified revolt as a form of mental illness, and torture can be considered as an implement of power, and liberty appears as a senseless dream.

Obedience is based upon orthodoxy which is grafted onto the individual. As Reich aptly noted:

"That a man steals because he is hungry, or that workers strike because they are being exploited, needs no further psychological clarification. In both cases ideology and action are commensurate with economic pressure. Economic circumstances and ideology coincide with one another. Reactionary psychology is wont to explain the theft and the strike in terms of supposed irrational motives; reactionary rationalizations are invariably the result. Social psychology sees the problem in an entirely different light: what has to be explained is not the fact that the man who is hungry steals or the fact that the man who is exploited strikes, but why the majority of those who are hungry *don't* steal and why the majority of those who are exploited don't strike. Thus, social economy can give a complete explanation of a social fact that serves a rational end, i.e., when it satisfies an immediate need and reflects and magnifies the economic situation. The social economic explanation does not hold up, on the other hand, when a man's thought and action *are inconsistent with* the economic situation, are *irrational,* in other words. The vulgar Marxist and the narrow-minded economist, who do not acknowledge psychology, are helpless in the face of such a contradiction."

(Wilhelm Reich, *The Mass Psychology of Fascism,* Pocket Books, New York, 1976:17).

Continual falsification of information constitutes another important characteristic of the system of *1984:* the State is in possession of absolute truth at every moment of its existence and it always has been. The facts seem to contradict it? Corners must be rounded off, modified, re-interpreted, even if they should say the opposite of what was previously promulgated.

Jeanine Verdès-Leroux (1984) deals with this subject and attributes to Stalin the idea of re-writing history in a new way and in the manner in which it must perforce be written. It must also be said that, faithful to his philosophical training, Marx tended towards determinism and, in his eagerness to discover the ultimate case of determination, he favoured determination outright, that which slumbers in the night of time and which will follow us till the end of the world. He was really the first not only to propose the re-writing of history, but to pretend to give it a scientific basis. What followed has merely been the application of this technique to the needs of the State and of politicians. Developing Stalin's thought at the Institute of Red Professors (red with anger? with pride?

with shame? with embarrassment? take your pick!), Kaganovitch explains what the history of the Bolshevik party must be: "It doesn't really matter what the authentic Bolshevik did or didn't do on such and such a date: Facts and documents must be interpreted in the light of current events." (Did Orwell say it any better? And to suggest that fiction scares us!) It becomes dangerous when facts no longer mean anything, when only the intentions and ambitions of the moment count. In the footsteps of Stalin, European communist parties have yielded to the temptation to destroy history and to re-write, no matter what they say. That has led them to defend some follies for which they bear responsibility.

The constant surveillance to which Eurasians were subjected used to be rather comical, but it is beginning to arouse anxiety today. Authorities want to see, and liberty consists in not being seen. Yet in this day and age, where can one hide? Against their will, unbeknown to them, without their permission, the State organs of information and others know all about the state of people's health, their solvence, their academic training, and their financial situation, etc. If need be, mail is opened, telephone conversations are tapped, and surveillance devices are installed in homes. And then the Canadian government wants to equip itself with a security agency to protect honest citizens from subversion! That means a general strike, a movement for separation by Québec. Society is under house arrest: we live in supervised freedom.

To be sure, this surveillance is carried out by means of the extensive action of the State affecting individuals, but that doesn't include the surveillance which people carry out on each other. Erich Fromm (1956) noted that in certain suburbs surveillance amongst peers is so strict that the slightest unusual behaviour entails rejection of the individual and his family on the part of the social environment. In the domain of work W.H. Whyte (1956) and R. Presthus (1962) arrive at the same conclusion: conformity pays more than originality.

Another instance of Orwellian foresight which totalitarian regimes never cease verifying is the use of torture. Physical torture is not new in history: all societies have practised it on foreigners, prisoners of war, and spies. Totalitarian regimes have, however, added an important variation: the use of medical and chemical means. One has to keep up with the times. The old methods of torture attacked the physical integrity of people, but left them free to think, even after having wrenched confessions out of them. The new methods, however, break the personality and subvert the emotions: they have formidable strength and the will can do nothing against them, because its own functioning is chemically blocked. Having presented the different stages in the evolution of torture in Chile as far as the military "coup d'état" is concerned, Ana Vasques (1984) concludes her article in the following manner:

"The application of torture is not an end in itself; one seeks, rather, an internalization of fear in order to arrive at self-censorship, which stifles all possibility of protest. If, on the face of it, the use of torture as government policy is redoubtable, the system which it supports is even more so."(205)

Another detail: torture no longer merely serves to obtain repentance or information from certain persons judged to be dangerous, but it is also aimed at citizens in general. Torture is no longer only applied to radical elements, but it also bears a message addressed to all members of a society: it has an exemplary character and a capacity for generalization. No one must feel safe, and that is the desired objective.

Another characteristic, which is a corollary to the preceding one: continual war and controlled revolt. Continual war never in fact affects the stability of the State: it is kept in the peripheral zones, far away, like the United States in Vietnam and the Russians in Afghanistan, at the same time as it serves to maintain the level of production. War thus does not merely constitute an end in itself: it is also the means used to control society and its members. It is a way to keep an eye on dangerous - i.e. insufficiently patriotic - people, and to dissipate the discontent which people might express regarding the kind of life which is imposed on them. War is a means of social control, and national security is the pretext by means of which the élite assure their hold on the body politic.

Since the time when George Orwell's novel was written sensibilities have changed, circumstances have been modified, and opinions are divided: does our world correspond to the one which the novelist foresaw or doesn't it? Has historical time caught up with poetic time, or have the two drawn apart? It is not easy to answer this question, but one thing is sure; we can already pick out certain manifestations of totalitarianism in our daily life.

"The withering away of civil society in favour of the State thus sets in motion the withering away of basic freedoms and the establishment of a pan-statist, more or less militarized society: we have assumed the habit of calling this sort of society 'totalitarian', because the State has totally supplanted civil society and has become the 'total State'. We have virtually achieved this stage. No action of local or professional, social or cultural concern can be undertaken by the interested parties themselves — even if they live in the same building — without interference, authorization, regulation or exemptions from a 'competent authority'. No initiative can be taken from below without the designation of someone who is responsible, not in respect to colleagues, but before the Law. No work can be done or undertaken if it is not given, that is to say predetermined in its nature and its heteronomous goal by an institutional 'employer'. No voluntary association can be formed without the 'institution' demanding accounts from it and without the political parties accusing it either of infringing upon their monopoly, or of not setting itself up within their orbit. Defined in his needs by a collection of institutions, of professions, of rules and of rights, the citizen is urged to behave as consumer and user, enjoying rights to a set of benefits, supplies and functions. S/he no longer consumes goods and services for which s/he feels an autonomous need, but those which correspond to the heteronomous needs which the professional experts of specialized institutions reveal to him/her." (Gorz, 1978:489).

Whence comes this thrust of Statism? For it is not new: it coincides with the appearance of capitalism. The supposed theory of 'laissez-faire' legitimized State intervention *de facto:* non-interference in the economy permitted entrepreneurs to make their fortune at the expense of the very health of the workers, and the exploitation was so terrible that it placed in danger not only their health, but also that of the whole of society. Consequently, when a crisis occurred, the State intervened again to refloat the faltering sectors of the productive system and to maintain peace with measures of social policy. From support as a temporary measure and from circumstantial aid as an initial subsidy, State intervention became decisive in economic development: the still celebrated theory of non-intervention is constantly belied by the facts, and even by those who still have the effrontery to profess it. In fact, the State became the essential cog-wheel and the principal creator of employment.

The capitalist system is going through a pretty difficult period, it must be admitted: perhaps it is not the final struggle, nor the ultimate crisis for which the Marxist-Leninists fervently pray, but Western societies are experiencing the most serious structural crisis since that of the years of the great depression. Capitalism is in the process of re-structuring, and the present situation is the natural development of the cult of the machine from the past century, only this time it threatens to keep its promise of delivering people from work by penetrating into the holy of holies, the pre-eminently human territory: decision-making. In the process of production human work risks becoming less and less important with the development of word processors, computers, micro-electronics, robots and other gadgetry. The most significant, as well as the most promising investments are being made in this sector, always with State aid, oddly enough: why walk on one's own two feet when one can use a docile crutch?

The development of machines hits exactly at the point where it hurts most, the tertiary sector. For the past few decades the number of workers employed in industry and agriculture has kept on shrinking; yet the State continued to absorb part of this work-force by extending its services. It appears, however, that data processing will "industrialize" the tertiary sector: clerical personnel, book-keepers, supervisors, everyone in the service sector will be affected by machines which will assume more and more complex tasks. Certainly the difficult economic situation is not favourable for employment, but assuredly, even if business picked up again, it is doubtful that workers would benefit from it: for the past twenty years the rate of unemployment has been edging upward, and it is difficult to see how the labour market could from one day to the next integrate the young people, the women who want to re-enter the work-force, the older people who want to keep on working, and recycled workers. The reason is simple: the economy can continue to develop without them.

The crisis through which we are passing is all the more profound as it affects the heart of our value system: work. Whereas in societies which have preceded us, work was considered as a means of assuring one's subsistence, in the capitalist system it has become a virtue associated with pride, independence, and vocation. It has not been so much work as such which has been extolled as the salary which was attached to it and which provided the means of survival, but the two have often been confused. And the virtue has been all the more lauded as the workers have begun to work for others as opposed to being self-employed. Even Marx went so far as to define work as the way for men to get in touch with nature. The Catholic church rallied to this position and the latest encyclicals sing the same tune. Those who run together end up getting together.

The current problem is colossal: now that wealth can be developed without human work, now that the capitalist dream is so close to being realized, namely to produce with docile machines which never baulk, which never unionize, what is to be done with the people who are left high and dry? Despite this reversal of orthodoxy, young people are still being pushed into specializing, but where can they betake themselves? No work, no income, but how can one continue to extol work when unemployment prevails? A terrible shock and a painful revision for capitalists and politicians: how does one replace the right to work by the right to an income? One wallows in a crisis of conscience. Poulantzas has described this position of Western democracies as authoritarian statism.

"We are witnesses to considerable modifications of the State in Western capitalist societies. A new form of State is in the process of being imposed: one would have to be quite blind (and passion, even if it stems from the noblest motives, is always blind) in order not to notice it. A form of State which I shall call, for want of a better term, authoritarian statism. A term which may indicate the general tendency of this transformation: the increasing monopolization, by the State, of the whole of socio-economic life hard upon the heels of the decisive decline of the

institutions of political democracy and of the draconian, and multifarious, restriction of those supposedly 'formal' liberties, the reality of which we discover, now that they are melting away. Although certain of these modifications have been under way for a long time, the present State represents a real turnaround in comparison with the preceding forms of the State."
(Poulantzas, 1978: 225-26).

The desire for power is the basis of the State: it is a well-known fact and an anarchist insight which political thinkers and practitioners have tried to forget. There has been a lot of talk about surplus value extorted by capitalism from the worker: the entrepreneur buys the work-force without paying the proper price for it, passing it off as just one element of production amongst so many others, when it is really the very touchstone of it. The same remark holds true for the politician who extorts power from the citizen: he is no more held to account than is the capitalist, and the vote, useful though it may be in certain situations, amounts to a periodic confiscation of social power for the benefit of a class of profiteers. Totalitarianism is therefore not an accidental phonomenon of history; it is quite simply the product of the development of the State, and any statified society may one day or another undergo the cruel experience, at the mercy of historical circumstances. How can one not understand the incisive criticism of power which Bakunin drew up, criticism which maintains its relevance across the years:

"We are in fact enemies of all authority, for we realize that power and authority corrupt those who exercise them as much as those who are compelled to submit to them. Under its baneful influence some become ambitious despots, lusting for power and greedy for gain, exploiters of society

117

for their own benefit or that of their class, while others become slaves."
(Maximoff, 1953:246)

Are we therefore condemned to live in a totalitarian society? Are we evolving irresistibly towards a harsher form of society? Some people think so, and nor are they wrong: as a social form of organization the State has demonstrated remarkable dynamism, to such a point that few societies exist without a State, and what is more, the intellect has difficulty imagining a destatified and free society. In any case, despite its strength and its cruelty, the State is an historical form, which has developed in particular circumstances and which can be modified at the behest of different circumstances: it all depends on theory, practice and feeling.

We are going through a period of social change in the course of which it is difficult to identify the new society. Besides, it has become more and more evident that the official theory of socialism, Marxism, lags behind practice. For a long time Marxism has served a dual function. On the one hand, it served as a base of operations for criticizing regimes making claim to socialism, and which set up Marxism as a sort of State religion: the theory served to demonstrate how the countries of the Eastern bloc foundered in ever so many deviations, and in what way these States had preserved some capitalist features which estranged them from socialism as planned. On the other hand, Marxism has been the weapon of numerous intellectuals for analyzing the implantation of capitalism in Asia, Africa and Latin America, where this mode of production assumed forms similar to those which had previously been familiar in Europe and the United States.

In the long run this criticism and the practice which accompanied it ended up having doubtful value: in fact, if Marxism continued to explain development elsewhere, it became less and less capable of understanding what was happening at home! An appropriate turn of events for a theory which advocated transcendence of the present situation, but a cruel affliction for the theoreticians in search of the absolute. The reason is quite simple: official Statist-Marxist socialism based its criticism on economic alienation and exploitation at the work-place, whilst the fundamental change which has occurred has been that of the "capitalization" of the entire society. Almost every sphere of society has been exposed to capitalist exploitation and transformed into merchandise, so that as alienation has progressed, the battle fronts have multiplied and the struggle has become more pronounced by taking on new forms. From this point of view the work site has remained the traditional place of resistance to capitalism, but it is no longer the only one, nor even the most advanced one. What features on the agenda of social change is not merely the end of economic exploitation, but indeed the end of exploitation itself. The expansion of the State and megacorporations illustrates once more, and in striking fashion, the necessity of getting rid of a social order which puts in danger the very existence of society.

Far from wasting away, the opposition movement has gathered strength and has assumed new forms, with the result that the official theory of social change has broken down into the practice of opposition movements which have loomed up in advanced capitalist societies. No surprise: the situation of the United States as well as that of European countries no longer corresponds to that of the nascent socialist movement. Other days other ways, and other theories.

It is becoming imperative to consider the change of Western societies as being of a qualitative nature and oriented towards the radical transformation of our way of life, towards a situation which is entirely different from what we have known up until now. Yet, in a period of searching and upheaval like that which the century has seen, it is normal that practice precedes theory and that conditions establish themselves before concepts indentify them. Marcel Rioux illustrates this period well with the concept of rupture:

> "Without excluding this meaning (epistemological rupture), the idea of rupture which we are using goes much further, insofar as it is meant to denote the discontinuity between social-cultural norms, be they of a type of society, of a social structure and class, or of a group, and the practices which 'really exist' in the thought, the action and the ways of those social entities. Beyond favouring practice as opposed to theory, this point of view tries to close in upon what is being hatched and what is trying to come forth in the midst of social groups for which certain norms have ceased to be operative." (1982:53).

Because of this explosion in the movement quite a few people jump to the conclusion that the movement is losing strength and that behind every breach in the unified movement lurks a CIA agent. (KGB abstaining). The real problem, however, does not lie there: it is that of a theory which connot give an account of a decentralized movement, congealed as it is in the structures of the First International, with its great large-scale movements and Statist tendency. We are therefore witnessing a desperate effort of Marxism to get back on track with feminism, and with popular and community groups, whilst history would have dropped it ages ago if it had not been for the efforts of intellectuals longer on memory than on imagination.

In the absence of a formal theory which would provide an account of the present situation, just as socialism managed to do from the end of the last century until after the second world war, so one must fall back upon experience, experimentation, practice and praxis, in order to try and disclose the new orientation of social change. From this point of view our epoch resembles that of the first half of the nineteenth century, which was a period of transition: that epoch continued to harbour the vestiges, and they were still important vestiges, of the Middle Ages, at the same time as the capitalist system was beginning to sprout and take off. And when one retraces the main ideas which were to constitute the spearhead of the socialist movement, one realizes that they were almost all formulated in the course of the first half of the last century, with the second half trying to find the way to put them into effect. One should therefore not be surprised to find a definite relationship between the aspirations of the alternative movement and the ideas conveyed by the movement which was subsequently and pejoratively referred to as utopian socialism.

This search for an alternative is not carried forward with an open and concentrated offensive under the command of a general staff, nor with a plan for society which is clearly enunciated and shared, nor with a unified theoretical vision: it is expressed, rather, by scattered and spontaneous instances of rupture and reconstruction wherever it is possible and important to act. This "movement" protests on occasion, to be sure, but it is above all engaged in drawing up, trying out, and acquiring for itself the maximum amount of autonomy possible in life, and that right now. In short, this search is carried out for the moment on the fringe, and is expressed in what is called the counter-culture, in popular movements of self-organization, in the manifold community and collective movements, which are always autonomous and innovative in comparison with the existing dominant practices of organizational, social, and individual life.

Social life stretches out on a continuum, of which it is possible to clearly identify the two poles. On the one hand, we can recognize the great socio-historical processes which seem to unfold extraneously to the individual and upon which s/he often has little immediate control: one only has to think of the arms race, industrial restructuring, or urbanization. If all the members of a given society decide to behave in a manner different from that which is expected of them, as happens in periods of revolution, for example, there ensues a greater identity between the individual will and the collective orientation. This identify is, however, never complete, nor is it desirable that it should be, for at the other pole of the continuum resides the individual, the person, who is at one and the same time the product of his/her environment and the productive element of society. Now in order to unfurl the great social processes mediation is required, unobstructed thoroughfares through which people are subjected to the forces of change at the same time as they influence them. The group is one of those mediating agencies where the social and the individual meet and interpenetrate.

The key role of this mediation does not merely consist of developing another kind of practice, which is very important, but also and above all, simultaneously of developing another sensibility. That is one of the themes which Bookchin constantly lays before us throughout his books, i.e. the necessity of developing another sensibility, of linking the social individual to the personalized society.

"What we crucially lack is the consciousness and sensibility that will help us achieve such eminently desirable goals — a consciousness and sensibility far broader than customarily meant by those terms. Our definitions must include not only the human ability to reason logically and respond emotionally in a human fashion; they must also include a fresh awareness of the relatedness between things and an imaginative insight into the possible." (Bookchin, 1982:19).

Even Marcuse (1969), having described with such cynicism the advent of one-dimensional man, ended up thinking that the logic of capital was not as tight as he had believed, and that the blossoming of a new sensibility could constitute the seed of change. In contrast to this tardy conversion, anarchists have always claimed that sensibility constitutes both a means of change as well as its results.

CONCLUSION

Does 1984 really resemble *1984*? Some people are tempted to subject the novelist's predictions to the test of reality and to deduce from that whether he was right or wrong. It would be well, however, to remember that George Orwell was not the only one to describe totalitarianism. Some years before him, in 1932, Aldous Huxley had published a novel decribing a totalitarian society based on science and technology. Everything had been foreseen by the State, from relaxation to amorous relationships, passing by way of production. Through drugs, genetic manipulation, and conditioning human beings are happy whilst responding perfectly to the needs of those in authority. Contrary to *1984* where torture is the foundation of social functioning, in *Brave New World* happiness is the rule.

Was Orwell or Huxley right? Probably both of them, for totalitarianism has developed simultaneously on the basis of fear and happiness. Certain systems use one more than the other, but none can do without fear, any more than it can do without happiness. Are we therefore condemned to live in fear and a false sense of happiness? Nothing could be less sure. The different social movements of Western societies lead one to believe that though the contest is a tough one, the outcome is not as clear as it seems. And as far as the regimes of the countries with real socialism are concerned, one can share this query with Lefort:

"And, in turn, I ask one question: what becomes of the Revolution — what has become of it — under the impetus of Jacobins and Bolsheviks — can one declare that no lesson could be drawn from it in the hypothetical case of a revolutionary uprising in our time? Or, to put it in other, surely preferable, terms: if a revolution broke out in a society which had assimilated into its structure the effects of Jacobinism and of Bolshevism, would it not benefit from the experience of the phenomenon of bureaucracy and would it not generate a new image of what is possible and what is impossible?" (1976:210)

translated by Robert Mayo.

Critical Dimensions of Orwell's Thought

by Jean Ellezam

George Orwell left his mark on an era, and many tributes have been paid him, justifiably, as a writer and as an outstanding individual. Unfortunately, however, these eulogies tend to ignore or diminish his originality as a socio-political thinker.

It is with a sense of urgency that this essay attempts to remedy the deficiency: first, by separating Orwell's work from other literature that looks into the future; second, by determining what Orwell foresaw about power structures in his ironic attacks on militant orthodoxy; and, finally, by evaluating the obsolescence of certain Orwellian conceptions in view of recent social change.

Orwell is generally associated with three types of futurist writing, with little understanding of how or why he differs from these genres. His work is as different from futurology (Herman Kahn, Daniel Bell, Alvin Toffler) as it is from genuine science fiction or from Huxley's biological extrapolation. He breaks away from each of these in carrying to the limit a transitional concept of science and technology. As a whole, literature that looks into the future makes a fetish of science. For Orwell, science depends principally on relationships between subjects, constituting a means to class power rather than an end in itself, indiscriminately beneficial.

Futurology

Fetishism takes many forms. Futurology ("future science") sees the essence of the problem in the precipitous nature of change, which disrupts people's ways of thinking and their mode of social adaptation. Such a premise leads this extrapolative genre into the moralizing and psychologizing themes of the "value crisis" — so often carried to a naive pseudo-humanism that shrinks from what Alvin Toffler calls the "chalenge of change". It is, of course, hardly possible that all the disruption inherent in "change" could be totally unrelated to the natural forces that make change necessary and, consequently, understandable.

Science fiction

A second model of reification is found in science fiction. This sub-type of adventure novel derives its energy from the sensational aspects of science. The psychological drama is limited to Promethean struggles between spectacular machines. Battles between objects or monsters make good theatre, but they ignore any real social relationship. The better novels offer variety, intensity, and complexity, and they succeed in being evocative to some degree; nonetheless, the scenario is a simplistic one in which the actors have become mere onlookers in a titanic conflict. Thus "tamed", the drama appeals to a very narrow range of emotions. Suspense can be created simply by inventing a more extravagant and perverse machine. Once the complexity of the social universe and its conflicts is destroyed, the object becomes the subject. A prison-like, caricatural world, peopled only by robots, then becomes possible. Since it is generally a matter of fleeing this hostile and dehumanized world — though one is never permitted to determine its structural origin — a military officer tends to be in charge of the escape or battle. Science fiction seems inevitably to imply the military and uses its hierarchical vocabulary. But the very personal and transhistorical qualities that elevate the hero to saviour suggest an inescapable universe over which he has no control. This literature can be enchanting, entertaining, or distressing, but its adversaries are fictitious, and it projects the imagination into a timeless, sterile Beyond.

To speak of tomorrows is to acknowledge the present, thus to conceive it. Futurology and science fiction are disturbing not because of any terror they reveal, but because of what they leave unsaid. The daring, fantastic concepts are remarkably shallow. Paradoxically, a lack of involvement prevails, since the structural origin of thought or actions is never linked to the nature of society and its inherent, concrete conflicts. The hero commands unanimity and internal solidarity by virtue of his perpetual struggle against an external enemy, visibly evil (dictator, criminal, sorcerer, rampaging robot). The unifying role of the evil external agent raises few questions. Contrary to appearances, the fantastic ignores the mediating role of science and technology in society, thus ratifying — without irony — a state of extreme reification.

The Orwellian brand of future-gazing resists these literary tendencies, condemning the mediation of knowledge and all attempts to mask its historicity. Orwell denounces the instrumentalization of technology and the externalization of adversity in order to achieve "internal peace" and harmony. He deplores the empty fiction of the magic hero, ascribing the unifying effect of a hero to the power structure. Similarly, the antagonism of power relationships results from the repressive self-discipline of the Party — the Party, however, presented as the champion of truth, of freedom, and of sharing. Orwell eliminates sentiment, but not at all because of the exclusiveness of technology: the telescreen of *Nineteen Eighty-Four* illustrates relationships, but it does not explain them. Psycho-sexual and ideological pressure creates a build-up of anxiety relationships — self-explanatory expressions of domination.

Biological extrapolation

Aldous Huxley illustrates the third type of fetishism — biological extrapolation. Critics like to compare Orwell's irony with that of Huxley, but these two essayists were radically different. Whereas Orwell saw the basis of the power structure in the socio-political sphere — the social arising from the social — Huxley ascribed the essential determining role to bio-physiological discoveries. The more complete the biological domination, the more harmonious the structure of the "best of all worlds". This "naturalism" derived from a literary credo which, in turn, was the result of a fascination with science and extravagant scientific discoveries. For Huxley, both man and the machine were products of biology, their capabilities automatically pre-selected, recorded, and directed. The automated individual, well integrated in his assigned class, is surrounded by a radiant, hedonist world where relationships are unencumbered by thought or anxiety. Huxley captivates, stimulates, but does so within the framework of a fantastic and fanciful escape into a future in which the social structure was perceived in terms of a self-regulation of which it was unaware. The biological dynamic could not be superimposed in any way upon the historical dialectic.

Aldous Huxley was the grandson of Thomas Henry Huxley, a well-known zoologist, a fervent Darwinist, and an active bourgeois reformer. In line with family tradition, Aldous received a primarily scientific education. Partially blinded in adolescence, the future author of *Brave New World* saw his own world fade; his inwardness and an inclination toward the fantastic intensified. First a poet, then a novelist and essayist, he became in India a mystic and student of Taoism, experimenting with drugs in an attempt to achieve higher spiritual communion.

Orwell's activism

Huxley's cautious, deliberate approach (order and cyclical regulation are achieved through biological contemplation) contrasts sharply with the activism of Orwell.

Orwell was the son of a low-level civil servant in India. With the help of scholarships, he was able to attend private schools, but he was intensely aware of his origins. His continual rebellion and political involvement were expressions of this early class shock. A deep hostility toward imperialism developed during his term as a police sergeant in Burma (*Burmese Days,* 1934). Back in Europe, he became personally acquainted with poverty *(Down and Out in Paris and London,* 1933). He wrote a social analysis of the plight of English miners hit by the recession (*The Road to Wigan Pier,* 1937), and was a night worker in a factory during the war.

Political activism had led him to fight in the Spanish Civil War, where he received a serious throat wound. Orwell's sympathies in this conflict lay at first with the revolutionary socialists of the Workers' Party, a group that was treacherously eliminated with the assent of the small minority which formed the Spanish Communist Party — numerically incapable of governing the country alone. In the face of repression, political assassination, and the internal quarrels and hypocrisy of the Communist party, Orwell became more radical. Having entered the Spanish Civil War a socialist, he left it an anarchist (*Homage to Catalonia,* 1938). The last decade of his short life (47 years), spent as a journalist, confirmed his uncompromising convictions, as well as his undeniable courage and rare strength of character.

Having been personally involved in great historical events, unlike Huxley, he attached less importance to the system of social control than to active resistance; he was preoccupied with the concept of disorder as an emancipatory force. Opposition is inherent in domination, and the novel *Nineteen Eighty-Four,* written in 1948 (four years after *Animal Farm,* which was published in 1945), is pervaded by a sense of activism. Orwell instinctively asserts that existence precedes essence.

Liberalism seizes on *Nineteen Eighty-Four* for justification. However, opposition to totalitarianism does not in any sense imply unconditional acceptance of the bourgeois world. There are other dualities besides capitalism *versus* socialism in the ideological spectrum; Manicheism is a poor model. Criticism of the Party can represent only a finite step along the scale of total rejection.

Criticism of the bourgeois system is evident, explicit or implicit, in all of Orwell's writing. He had suffered too much from that system to suddenly become its apologist. This is why his popular image as a liberal is paradoxical. Nonetheless, in this year when Orwellian prophecies are being so keenly scrutinized, the sensationalism of the mass media has seized upon just that image. Orwell never lost faith in the proletariat, believing it to be invincible by the very nature of the power structure which made it an object of submission. Work is not only a matter of action, but of being.

The Proles were immortal... In the end their awakening would come. And until that happened, though it might be a thousand years, they would stay alive against all the odds, like birds, passing on from body to body the vitality which the Party did not share and could not kill.
Nineteen Eighty-Four (1983): Penguin Books Ltd., p. 188.

Orwell differed from another of his Darwinist precursors, Herbert G. Wells. This famous author of *The Time Machine* (1895), *The Invisible Man* (1897), and *The War of the Worlds* (1898), belonged to the school of socialist elitism. He advocated the abolition of

Nations, and planetary government by what he called the "Universal State", ruled by a mandarinate of experts and technicians. For Wells, only the middle class, by virtue of its competence, could be a revolutionary force — not the proletariat. Consequently, he preached the abolition of the "demagogic democracy" which maintained that all individuals are equally well endowed with nature's gifts. Orwell, by contrast, distrusted all dominating authority. As his weapon of attack, he preferred rather an incisive critical irony in the style of Jonathan Swift, the 18th-century satirical polemicist who felled ministers with a stroke of his pen.

Political content of the critique

Orwellian iconoclasm attacked the forms of alienation inherent in the sexual sublimation, militant asceticism, and terrorism (intellectual as well as physical) of Marxism. With violent invective, he railed against the loss of social historicity, which precluded any basis for identification and resulted in a distorted world: perfectly homogeneous, without vertigo or otherness, it was a world immobilized by permanent amnesia. The loss of memory had to be active, however, and co-exist with an unconditional and deliberate acceptance of values. Discourses and facts were falsified, and civil records suppressed; statistics were altered retrospectively in order to stimulate desired reactions.

Thus, "Doublethink" enabled fiercely hostile feelings and ideas to overlap without ever clashing. The mind storing contradictory data, two independent lines of thought each received their own information. Fortunately, the impoverishment of the language, thanks to "Newspeak", limited the content of the thought lines. According to the new language, a thing was or was not; all middle ground, all nuance, had been erased.

> What sense is there in having a whole string of vague, useless words like 'excellent' and 'splendid' and all the rest of them? 'Plus good' covers the meaning, or 'doubleplus good', if you want something stronger still.
> *Nineteen Eighty-Four,* p. 48

The implacable pragmatism of "Newspeak" had the additional advantage of eliminating all superfluous sentiment. Such feelings were extinguished, since there were no words for them. The dual functionality of language achieved its goal.

Today's impoverishment of language and the lack of dialogue, accentuated by the omnipresence of television, turn each individual into the consumer of a monopolized and unidirectional culture. The broad normative tolerance of individuals in the modern capitalist state stifles any passionate rebellion. The troubles of daily life glance off a protective shell. The technostructure is adept at separating the rational from the affective, lending credibility to much of Orwell's vision of Doublethink. The thought lines remain distinct and parallel.

The State and *Nineteen Eighty-Four*

Two significant aspects of the State captured Orwell's attention. The first is that the State is an absolute point of reference, and therefore transcendent, existing independently of the individuals who hold power. It is a common symbol of the exercise of global power, created by the demands of society. Like God, it cannot be known or seen. It can only be "revealed". Thus, the State in *Nineteen Eighty-Four* judiciously "revealed" itself in the mystic and evanescent figure of Big Brother. The supreme authority defines itself according to circumstances, as the need for communication arises.

This explains, on the other hand, why the State is the embodiment of concrete power relationships. To construct in an objectified praxis (borrowing a term from Karel Kosik) an instrument for the use of power, in acquiring its true "objectness" — what Marxism would call its "materialism" — this abstract model, corresponding to real statuses and operational ideas, must be corroborated by discourses, social *conceptions* of the dependence relationship. It must be precisely "revealed", that is, made explicit by the language experts. An existing mechanism of persuasion is used to portray the State as the expression of the collective interest. In *Nineteen Eighty-Four,* consensus was extracted by presupposing a common will.

Without obligatory participation, the "dialogue" between the State and its citizens would be shown up for what it is, an authoritarian monologue. These citizen-spectators must believe they have a voice in the political process. The State must remain "the people", or lose its transcendent nature. Open debates, the parliamentary game, and the rules of information are all indispensable to the "public" nature (Habermas uses the term *"publicité"*) of the State. This "publicness" could not have been better achieved than through the figure of Big Brother. The Father falls victim to his own external nature; a Big Brother avoids this difficulty. Such family-like responsible egalitarianism is more accessible than an authoritarian paternalism.

The transcendent character of the State depends on the existence of a villain: in this case, Goldstein, the devil's henchman, the eternal foreign enemy, perpetually in quest of conspiracies. As menacing as he was, he proved extremely useful to the internal functioning of the system. Evil is as structuring as Good, since one authorizes the meaning of the other. These are two sides of the same coin.

Information and the State

At once symbol and self-constituting entity, the State is by its very nature implicated in the whole issue of information. In fact, it is precisely through information that the particular character of the "Communist" world (to use this abusive label) is best revealed. Orwell's vision is unequivocal. Coercive relationships are defined by their opposites. The word "justice" is, after all, applied to something which is a mere parody of justice; the "Ministry of National Defence" is a bloody forum of aggression. And the French Republic inscribes her façades with the cold irony of the slogan "Liberty, Equality, Fraternity"?

The "Communist" world is based on neither the rules of the capitalist market nor the strictly economic conventions of free enterprise. The socio-political features of any State's power system are the structural determinant. Orwell's novel applies so well to the "Communist" world because its essence lies in the area of information. If the structure of privilege, that is to say, the proximity to the techno-bureaucratic apparatus, explains the rules of economic circulation and its management, the economy itself is a consequence of the State. If the State has such a power, it must be protected from transcendence. Everything depends on this, just as the hereditary castes of times past revolved around eternal symbolico-religious activity. The Communist totalitarian State is, itself, aware of its absolute centrality, an aspect which it has cultivated since the time of Lenin. Attacks against the State shake it to its very core. Such a fragile system does not branch out into all areas of society, as does capitalism, for example, through a complex network of individual business contracts — which, in fact, forms the basis of the social fabric.

The central State avoids this complicated entanglement. Its world operates mechanically; it is almost exclusively subordinate to political power and, consequently, to its repressive nature. The structure of privilege originates outside itself. It calls for symbolic persuasion rather than techno-economic competence, which is why drastic control of information is so necessary. The structuring power resorts to denunciations, espionage, and secret police. It is therefore preoccupied with the control of language and communications. In such a system, lying becomes necessary and, as a result, disconcerting — to paraphrase the Soviet dissident, Anton Ciliga.

Since the appeal to order cannot be supported, as in the capitalist State, by threat of exclusion from certain areas of the system (unemployment, marginalization), the totalitarian State has no recourse but to exclude offenders from the entire system (imprisonment, torture, deportation) — unless it attempts psychiatric "re-education", a form of violence of which *Nineteen Eighty-Four* gives but a caricature. Dissidence is a concrete danger, to which the techno-bureaucratic gerontocrats in power respond with sinister "Communist" reprisals. Dissidence disrupts the well-oiled mechanisms of information control, the very essence of the Communist State. It directly attacks the State, of which every minor plant manager is a representative. Thus, there is no army of mediators to maintain liaison with the central authority, as is the case elsewhere. Such mechanisms are the reverse of the system of free information, which occasionally draws on dissidence to renew itself. Advertising in the West points up these differences. There is a close relationship between advertising and the product it markets; advertising exerts an influence on the product itself. In the East, propaganda takes the place of advertising. Since there is absolutely no competition between products, propaganda is devoted to selling national heroes and the Party. There is an undeniable relationship between propaganda and the Great Man, since his power seems to derive from personal authority.

The preponderance of the middle class in the structural relationships of domination

The issue of information calls into question the status and the role of the middle class. Word manipulators promote the "publicness" of the system:

> The new aristocracy was made up for the most part of bureaucrats, scientists, technicians, trade-union organizers, publicity experts, sociologists, teachers, journalists, and professional politicians. These people, whose origins lay in the salaried middle class and the upper grades of the working class, had been shaped and brought together by the barren world of monopoly industry and centralized government. As compared with their opposite numbers in past ages, they were less avaricious, less tempted by luxury, hungrier for pure power, and, above all, more conscious of what they were doing and more intent on crushing opposition.
> *Nineteen Eighty-Four,* p. 177.

One of these word manipulators was a member of the Party, a militant who was both ascetic and orthodox: "In a Party member... not even the smallest deviation of opinion on the most unimportant subject can be tolerated." (*Nineteen Eighty-Four,* p. 181). In fact, the purity of one's orthodoxy was measured by the degree of perversion, and the asceticism applied only to certain individuals. Three worlds existed: that of the Inner Party, characterized by privilege and authority; that of the Outer Party of administrative subalterns who excelled at text-handling; and that of the Proles, who were untouched by government directives. They lived "as free as animals" — Orwell deliberately uses the condescending epithet the Party used to describe them. Previously, such condescension had been masked by excessive veneration of the proletarian on the part of the intellectual.

Orwell's vision rings true. The doctrinaire intellectual is committed only to setting an example. He is motivated by an inner conviction of Good, purity being more important to him than the need for existence *per se*. For him, attitudes and behaviour result less from a contradictory mode of existence, born of conflict, than from a "scientific" and genuinely materialistic conception of it. Ideas are more important than the individual. A dialectical materialist takes pride in analyzing structures instead of interrelationships, which he considers somewhat too psychological. Paradoxically, however, he concentrates on order and contemplation, rather than movement and action — and ends up embracing the very principles of behavioural functionalism he had rejected.

The violent irony with which Orwell attacked the intellectual arose out of his own experience. The trauma of the Spanish Civil War inspired in him a lasting contempt for the middle class. Spanish Fascism took its recruits from the middle class, but then, so did the Catalonian Communist Party. It is hardly surprising that their doctrines were so similar.

Joseph Gabel lists the following common doctrines and practices:

... nationalism, militarism, the glorification of work, obsession with the records of economic production, the publicly proclaimed need to promote the attainment of social objectives, birth rate policies, the desire to "educate" youth by mass demonstrations, the domination of a single Party, unconditional admiration for the national leader, etc.[1]

According to Lenin's post-revolutionary thinking, social life was subordinate to the Party and, therefore, to the State. The slogan of Mussolini's Fascists ex-

137

pressed the same principle: "All in the state, nothing against the state, nothing outside the state".

The similarity extends to the totalitarian conception of art. After the effervescence of Russian and Italian futurism, Stalin and Mussolini began in the 1930s to restore order, the former with socialist realism, the latter with a crude return to ancient Rome: two types of allegorical art, well suited to promoting the cult of the personality and the centrality of power.

Mussolini was at first a leader in the Italian Socialist Party, and a radical Communist intellectual, editor of the avant-garde newspaper *l'Avanti*. It is less well known that Palmiro Togliatti, the general secretary of the Italian Communist Party, signed in August 1936, with all the members of his central committee, an unequivocal appeal for collaboration:

The Communists adopt the fascist programme of 1919, which is a programme of peace, liberty, defence of the rights of the workers... We proclaim that we are ready to fight, with you and with the Italian people, for the realization of the fascist programme.[2]

In Spain, the few doctrinaire communists became agents in the pay of the Comintern and its dreaded secret police, the Tcheka (forerunner of the K.G.B.). Left holding the reins of power, after bloody fighting that eliminated the Anarchists, they held the revolutionary movement in check by subordinating it to the war. Their brief rule was punctuated by numerous political assassinations within the movement.

The Anarchists had been clamouring for *immediate* collectivization and different forms of life. Once again, libertarian federalism challenged authoritarian centralism. There were echoes of this confrontation in the past: in 1919, when the German social democracy of Ebert, Scheidemann, and Noske destroyed the Spartacus movement (Rosa Luxemburg, Karl Liebknecht)[3]; in 1920, in Italy, when the Socialist Party and the Labour Confederation delivered the factory councils into the hands of the Fascists; and in 1921 in Russia, when Lenin's Bolshevists crushed the *makhno* movement and the Kronstadt rebellion. In all of Europe, as in Hungary, similar movements are developing. These movements spring from a common doctrinal history which transcends national borders. Social democratic centralism and organized trade unionism continually repress polycentric and polysemic grassroots movements: elsewhere and tomorrow, or here and now.

Limit of reification

A contemporary of the Moscow trials and the Great Purges, Orwell had reason to be alarmed, and militant orthodoxy cause for worry. However, Orwell's alarm was premature. Although Winston, the protagonist of *Nineteen Eighty-Four,* ended up loving Big Brother, the subject was never fully objectified. Reification cannot be complete, since History would automatically cease for lack of subjects. The abolition of the subject would mean the end of society. It is useless to envisage an automatized non-humanity among men; it would be nothing but pure functionalism, a technology of artificially animated objects. Even artificiality, as "artifact", requires an articulator-subject, and therefore a human alterity, unless one becomes God, and lives alone among the dead. All control of behaviour requires a controller, and hence a corresponding social structure — Robinson died. Orwell was aware of this; Winston proclaimed his emotions in the face of constant negation. They were indispensable; without them, the novel would have been stillborn. The spectre of the "end of the political state" and of the abolition of conflict relationships, precluding any axiological instability, remains problematic.

Orwell's parodies become more significant with the passage of time. He portrayed vividly new forms of transmission of power, whereby co-optation replaced heredity; he ridiculed the technocratic dream of stopping history; he studied the evanescent Big Brother authority figure; he added to the body of existential thought — and a good deal more. However, if his penetrating socio-philosophical analyses give an accurate picture of repression, further study of its evolution must be undertaken. The way is open for symbolic persuasion. Psychology is its modern manifestation: it is becoming the science of new coercive relationships.

New forms of power and its contradictions

Language experts today are less preoccupied with doctrinaire content of conceptual purity than they are with the form itself of thought and its adaptability. Without the restrictions of content — always considered contradictory and too demonstrative — the social sciences are free to study all facets of daily reality. They can investigate, from a therapeutic standpoint, an infinite variety of modes of behaviour, from sexual mores to group dynamics. No longer is the old idea of the quest for Good used to justify the invasion, but rather, efficiency and functionality. All the social sciences are being pervaded by psychology (sociology, sexology, education, industrial relations, social work) — to escape it, their only alternative is to devote themselves to pure scientific formalism.

Persuasion by torture, as portrayed in *Nineteen Eighty-Four,* is a last resort in capitalism today, accommodating itself between the realities of relatively free information and indifference. It is less useful to describe the repressive system of capitalist States, as it would dangerously weaken the democratic ideologies of freedom and equality, already shot through with contradictions. Today, norms appear as spontaneous urges, seemingly arising out of the "nature of things". Indeed, the social sciences have acquired greater legitimacy by becoming mundane. Good and Evil have departed the lofty realms of Heaven and come down to earth, where they are employed in the evaluation of "good" or "bad" attitudes, of adequate behaviour. No longer is there a formal point of reference that can assure absolute universality. But this gain is made at the cost of a frantic, empty relativism that lends itself to anguish and a need for structure. If any behaviour is acceptable, and the harsh but structuring adversity of the past is removed, the individual becomes his own point of reference. He feels solely responsible for his decisions, and his "self-realization", the touchstone of psychology.

The social sciences, however, represent a contradiction. Although they promote the integration and harmony of the rational and the emotional, they also call into question authority, communication, and leadership. On the other hand, they exaggerate the natural contradictions of the authority of capital which provoke changes in work expectations and, consequently, more drastic opposition. Going beyond the purely psychologizing aspect of therapy dealing with the mere *perception* of things, hostility spreads to all work relationships (for example, the partition of labour), and results eventually in the compartmentalization of life. In the workplace, on the one hand, the individual is expected to be rational, shrewd, and anonymous; in his personal life, on the other hand, he must show emotion, be feeling, giving. He is constantly torn between the two extremes. It is not a question of evoking the absolute transparence of individuality, but rather, of being aware of how parts of life that were formerly integrated are now fragmented. The lines of thought become tangled. Either the individual expresses affection in the work place, or rationality diminishes his pleasure in emotional, sexual and family life.

Thus, the healthy spontaneity demanded by the social sciences encounters a multitude of constraints, often naively defined in terms of the unalterable evidence of life in society, necessarily shaped by compromise. Satisfaction is not achieved through an act of the will, but through a total change in society; this is especially true since the impetus for change can originate only with the oppressed.

Conclusion

The type of behaviourism criticized in *Nineteen Eighty-Four* has become reality, but it takes more sinister forms than Orwell ever imagined. The capitalist system exercises its own persuasive power. The structure of relationships requires itself to be self-controlling; the rest is a matter for psychology. Countries of the Centre tend to depend less and less obviously on the display of force, at the risk of increasing violence in countries of the Periphery. Totalitarianisms vary in subtlety.

Translated by Josette Davenport
Edited by Natalie Laine

NOTES

[1] Joseph Gabel, "Le fascisme", *Encyclopedia Universalis* (Paris), vol. 6, p. 937.
[2] Palmiro Togliatti, *Appel aux Fascistes* (Paris: 1936), 64 pages.
[3] Note that Franz Mehring called the officers who arrested and assassinated Luxemburg and Liebknecht "the most brilliant minds that Marxism has produced since Karl Marx".

Orwell and Anarchy in 1984

by Frank Harrison

Like all utopias and anti-utopias, George Orwell's *1984* selected certain socio-political trends, and drew an imaginative picture of the kind of state and society that might develop should they become dominant. He was, of course, writing in 1948, three years after the end of the Second World War, and at the beginning of the Cold War. The military domination of the USA and the USSR in international relations was becoming obvious, as was the conflict between the two for the forseeable future. The lines were drawn for a propaganda battle of global proportions, which has continued down to the present day, keeping us aware of the constant threat to destroy us all through an escalation into a hotter war of thermo-nuclear destruction.

Even then, people not hypnotized by the rhetoric of either East or West (each in its own way claiming the mantle of true democracy), were concerned with the way in which this condition of permanent conflict influenced internal political developments. As early as 1945 the American libertarian, Dwight MacDonald, was warning us against the "Organic State." He argued that this concept of the state, already dominant in Germany and Russia, was making significant progress in Western countries also. Faced with external enemies, real or imagined, governments were demanding that the thoughts and actions of everyone be in accord with the policies of their rulers. The individual was given no significance except as part of that greater whole, the state. He wrote,

"... the theory is convenient for those in power on two scores: internally, it preserves the ladder of hierarchy, making rebellious behavior treason not only to those in authority but also to the alleged common interests of everybody, to what is reverently termed 'national unity' these days; in times of war, it makes it possible to treat the enemy population as a homogeneous single block, all of them equally wicked and detestable."[1]

He also argued that the theory was in correspondence with "the real arrangement of things in the modern world."[2] He hoped that the "long and honorable tradition of lawlessless and disrespect for authority"[3] which he saw in America might provide some protection against this development; and we must judge for ourselves concerning whether or not his hope was realized.

The point to be made, however, is that what MacDonald called "the Permanent War Economy" emerging from the Second World War, and the domination of the individual by the state which was found with it, were critically identified. Orwell also identified them, and extrapolating from them, wrote a novel about it.

As a journalist, Orwell was conscious of the power of instruments of communication, of the media. Recognizing that words can possess both critical and conformist characteristics, he shows us in *1984* a controlled system of communications using an absolutely uncritical new vocabulary, called Newspeak. A strictly functional vocabulary, Newspeak has no value-laden words which can expand the imagination and allow the individual to consider the possibility of alternative realities. Newspeak is an affirmation of the present. Words like Peace and Freedom lose all meaning through the enforced identity with their opposites. The slogans which symbolize the system are, War is Peace, Freedom is Slavery, and Ignorance is Strength. With this "doublethink", said often enough, reiterated in mindless reinforcement, in a system of controlled information, alternatives are denied. An uncritical acceptance of actual conditions, and the power relations which they sustain, is the result.

Orwell's other principal concern in *1984* is the modern state bureaucracy. That state, as we all can see, has cut itself adrift to a considerable extent from the economically-defined class structures of social life. To the extent that the individuals involved in the state, employed and paid by the state, are isolated from particular class interests, they become a group apart from the rest of society. The purpose of the average bureaucrat is to operate according to hierarchical rules, and to promote the interests of the organization. Orwell emphasizes this tendency by asserting that his future state has already destroyed private property. Given that, there are only the governors and the governed — the latter being the "proles." The purpose of those involved in politics becomes, simply, the getting and usage of power — for its own sake. The autonomous and bureaucratic interests of those who run the state become absolute and unqualified. The state's *raison d'être* becomes not a class, and not a specific moral goal towards which citizens must be persuaded and coerced, but the perpetuation of the state itself.

Thus we see that Orwell seized upon two identifiable features, present in both communist and non-communist societies, which seemed to be of increasing significance in the Cold War world of 1948. These were: 1) the control of language and opinion, and 2) the growth in the size and authority of the state. These became the core of his dead-end Nowhere (Utopia) which is his 1984 state of Oceania. Together they provide the foundation of an "organic state" such as was postulated and feared by perceptive minds like that of Dwight MacDonald. The television screens that watch over the actions of much of the population, the denial of spontaneous sexual and emotional relationships, and the material and spiritual poverty of the environment, are all but aspects of the all-consuming system which is characterized by the term Big Brother.

On the other hand, let us remind ourselves that Orwell was writing a novel, not giving a scientific or sociological prediction. In so doing, he was isolating features of modern societies which offended his political sympathies. Those sympathies were both anarchist and socialist in their orientation. *1984* is, therefore, best viewed not as a prediction, but as a warning to socialists concerning significant questions which they must face — in addition to property, exploitation, and class domination.

The warning is well taken, and should be. In western capitalist societies there are many evidences of what amounts to the monopolistic tendency of the state in areas of social control. It is true that leading state persons are known to be linked by economic, social and family ties to other elites (which is not the case in Orwell's Oceania). Yet the state's independent interest and capacity create a common opinion is substantial; and those who do not fall within its boundaries are named, numbered and filed by the police. A principal task of the police in both Canada and the USA is to keep a record not only of those who break the written law, but also of those who voice an extra-parliamentary criticism and challenge to the structure and policies of the state. The micro-chip and the modern computer have made this task all the easier. Thereafter, our dissidents have their phones tapped, their mail intercepted, their movements across national borders inhibited, and their employment opportunities blocked by both police intervention and the unwillingness of public and private employers to take on anyone who challenges the *status quo*. Where unemployment is endemic, particularly amongst the young, the personal costs of challenge become high. We should not wonder that university students have swallowed their bile of late. Criticism carries a high price when measured in the currency of job opportunities. Meanwhile, the language and orientation of the media continue to discourage alternate modes of thought and behaviour. It is, after all, 1984!

II

Orwell stressed characteristic features of the modern state, as a state, irrespective of its ideological and economic bases. The tendency today, however, is to presume that Orwell's imagery is principally a reflection and criticism of the USSR and other countries ruled by Marxist-Leninists. Indeed, the book is still banned in those countries, a fact which might be taken to support such a conclusion.

What is of particular concern to the ideological authoritarians of communism, what reminds them so much of their own system, can be summarized in the following features of Orwell's Oceania (a super-state composed of the USA, the UK, Australasia and South Africa):

1) The society is dominated by The Party, in the same way that the Communist Party monopolizes political power in the USSR.

2) Under the guidance of The Party, the state controls the economy, as it does every other aspect of the social condition.

3) The society is one which suffers from poor housing and consumer deprivation.

4) It is a society where there are political trials of those who oppose the policies of the state.

5) There is no rule of law — Orwell saying, no law at all. There can be arbitrary arrest by the Thought Police of anyone who is intellectually opposed to the régime.

147

6) Big Brother, a god-like figure removed from the population, could be thought to reflect the glorification of Stalin under the extremes of the "personality cult."

7) The arch-enemy of the regime, Goldstein, is a figure very much like Trotsky (whose real name, as we all know, was Bronstein).

These are all elements which remind us certainly of the Soviet Union of Orwell's time, a country dominated by Stalin from 1928 to 1953. Even the details of police procedure and incarceration suffered by *1984's* principal character, Winston Smith, echo the style of Stalin's police state under the domination of the NKVD. When Winston is in jail, for example, he notices "the astonishing difference in demeanour between the Party prisoners and the others. The Party prisoners were always silent and terrified, but the ordinary criminals seemed to care nothing for anybody... The positions of trust were given only to the common criminals, especially to the gangsters and the murderers, who formed a sort of aristocracy. All the dirty jobs were done by the politicals."[4] This is exactly the kind of thing that we are used to hearing about prisons and labour camps in Stalin's GULAG — that acronym for the State Labour Camp Administration brought into common parlance by Solzhenitsyn's trilogy. Dissidents, the thought criminals, were treated more harshly than ordinary criminals.

Similarly, after imprisonment, torture, and constant questioning, Winston was ready to confess to anything and everything. "He became simply a mouth that uttered, a hand that signed, whatever was demanded of him. His sole concern was to find out what they wanted him to confess, and then confess it quickly, before the bullying started anew."[5] The end product in the communist reality was the show trial, the pseudo-legal self-immolation and sentencing of destroyed personalities. In the thirties such famous Old Bolsheviks as Kamenev, Zinoviev and Bukharin went through this process in the USSR. At the time that Orwell was writing, the new People's Democracies of

Central Europe were gearing up to copy their master's model. Such show trials were, however, only for the important and symbolic few, beneath which there were millions of nameless citizens coerced and/or incarcerated for their supposed and real nonconformities. Orwell's character is just such a nameless soul, and perhaps his fate was even worse than those dragged off unwillingly by the security police. Losing every vestige of free will, Winston lost his humanity, and came to love Big Brother.

It might be argued that, even if Orwell's 1948 criticism of the Marxist-Leninist states was justified, things have changed; that the socialist systems of 1984 have rejected Stalinism, with its personality cult, police state, and a standard of life which is denied improvement by investment policies which emphasize heavy industry and the military. After Stalin's death, was not his last police chief, Beria, executed, and the police hierarchy itself thoroughly purged? Were not thousands rehabilitated, their crimes admitted as being nonexistent, their names published in *Pravda* and *Izvestia*? Has not Stalin been condemned, his body removed from the Lenin mausoleum?

Yet none of this can persuade us that Orwell's imagery no longer applies to the USSR or its political acolytes. At its very best it still must be regarded as a mere reformed Stalinism, with his heirs hysterically afraid of anything that threatens the control of all values by the communist party. Unofficial publications *(samizdat)* and their producers are repressed by the KGB, and dissidents are incarcerated according to spurious clauses in the criminal code. Military expenditures still make all but the most privileged undergo consumer deprivation; making *any* small town in North America a veritable consumer paradise compared with *any* Soviet city. A bureaucratic one-party state, demanding unquestioning obedience from both subordinate officials and citizens alike, isolating the leadership behind the closed doors of Central Committee and Politburo meetings, seems unwilling to accept any change which would alter the centralized structure of power. *Pravda* and *Izvestia* continue to publish the official slogans before all public celebrations, covering their front pages, and ready for copying on the banners of the carefully organized cohorts of the system who organize mass demonstrations into expressions of support for the Party. The list goes on; and it is certainly not difficult to see the chief features of Orwell's *1984* in the contemporary Soviet (and other communist-ruled) states.

To follow such a line of argument, however, to concentrate upon the USSR as a model for Orwell's *1984,* then or now, is to miss the critical breadth of his orientation. We should note that Orwell was writing about something which he called English Socialism (Ingsoc), not Bolshevism. In his image of a 1984 world, Bolshevism had ceased to exist. It has become Neo-Bolshevism, the ideology of Eurasia in the tripartite division of the world between three superpowers (Oceania, Eurasia and Eastasia). In his 1984 the state and the power structures associated with it had become far more important than the ideologies which justified them *for all three super-states.* Irrespective of ideology, each of the three was a functional copy of the others, with no difference between them. Orwell was presenting what has come to be called a "convergence theory." For him all states, whatever they called themselves, were heading in the same direction; and that direction was one in which the individual had less and less meaning or significance.

Part of this general distrust of state power (including, but not especially, that of the USSR) was Orwell's refusal to be associated with any specific ideology. What can be seen as an anarchistic distrust of all states is combined with an anarchist rejection of all-embracing theories. It is significant that the only ideological criticism of the state in *1984* is presented through the writings of the rebel, Goldstein (who does not even appear as a character); and that Goldstein's book is provided for Winston by a servant of the state hierarchy, O'Brien, who becomes Winston's torturer. In this manner, Orwell distanced himself from a formal ideological position. Like Bakunin in the nineteenth century, he seems to have mistrusted ideology as a basis for an intellectual repression, with a new "priesthood" of ideological leaders forcing everyone into their own model of perfection, their own Procrustean bed.

Ideologies, as world-views which seek to co-ordinate the ideas and actions of large groups of individuals, possess a capacity to deny the significance of the individual. We have all seen how general combinations of ideas, going under the title of nationalism, communism, fascism, etc., have justified the sacrifice of individual human beings to a grand design explained in terms of intellectual abstractions. Structures of authority are reinforced by the voluntary and enthusiastic obedience of the adherents of an ideology to its promoters. At the same time, the followers are encouraged to lose their own sense of worth, well-being, and autonomy. The ideology comes to deny independent thought and criticism, and becomes a framework for an automatic response of the believer to the leader, without thought, without reason, without even a modicum of common sense. Individuals thereby become a yelping mob of thoughtless respondents to the calculated phrase of their leaders — as when Maggy Thatcher screamed nationalism to the British during the Falklands War, arranged for the deaths of a few soldiers, and won an overwhelming victory in the general election shortly afterwards.

At a more general level, any number of value-laden terms can be used to stir the emotions, rather than the minds, of a population. We have "hurrah" words like democracy and freedom; and "boo" words like communist and anarchist. Such is the power of this ideological conditioning that it continues as a central feature of the continuation of all political systems, dependent on the mindlessness of their inhabitants. One group of Dutch libertarians presented it as follows, discussing the perpetuation of the capitalist state:

"Indeed, far from rebelling, the workers continued to work hand in glove with the capitalists. In wartime they showed themselves willing to die in droves at the behest of the capitalists. And, in peacetime, the workers cooperated to the extent of backing the imprisonment of fellow working-class people found guilty by ruling-class courts of 'petty' 'illegal' capitalist acts such as thievery and bank robbery, while the biggest thieves of all — the capitalists — were accorded great prestige, wealth and privileges for their large-scale crimes committed openly every day of the year."[6]

We are reminded of Diogenes the Cynic who, upon seeing a thief chased from the temple by priests, asked, "Why are the big thieves chasing the little thief?" The answer is that the received values of an authoritarian ideology persuade us to maintain a double standard which legitimizes the powerful. It is Doublethink.

In *1984* the direction of public emotion by key words and phrases is revealed as the fundamental purpose of political ideology. This can occur as much under a socialist economic system as any other. As a socialist Orwell was concerned to show this, and to warn that socialism might be side-tracked through the control of ideas by a statist élite. Meanwhile, the manipulative capacity of the state is presented as being so strong that, when Oceania suddenly changes sides in the perpetual military conflict, its population responds immediately: "One minute more, and the feral roars of rage were again bursting from the crowd. The Hate continued exactly as before, except that the target had been changed."[7] Orwell's own example might have been the way in which public attitudes towards the USSR were altered following the end of the Second World War. Smiling Uncle Joseph became, after a short time, that evil Dictator Stalin. On the other side of the coin the Western Allies soon became capitalist imperialists for the communists. And today, in 1984, we are witness to the amusing turnabout in American relations with China, with Ronald Reagan clasping the hand of Communist China's Premier. During the Vietnam War, China was a threat to all of Asia; and during his 1980 election campaign Reagan was just as vitriolic. In sum, we see that historical events may move more slowly than literary events, taking years rather than minutes, but the conclusion is the same. Policies change, and public opinion is manipulated to support them, in whatever political system you happen to reside.

We can conclude, therefore, that the fundamental question of Orwell's novel is not, "What is wrong with socialism?" Rather, the question is, "What is wrong with the state as a political mechanism?" — whatever the structures of government, whatever the nature of property therein. *1984* is properly seen as a reaffirmation of the anarchism with which Orwell had been fascinated ever since the Spanish Civil War, and of which he wrote in *Homage to Catalonia*. In this anti-utopia which he outlines for us, he is saying that the state — even a socialist state — is in itself possessed of such capacities of control that all autonomy can be denied. In so doing, he raised the level of inquiry above the sterile categories of Marxism, and beyond the simplistic "them/us" perception of international politics.

Not anti-socialist, but anti-state socialist, *1984* holds a warning against a dehumanization which exists to a degree in every modern state, and which is characterized by a pure will to power. Power as a self-subsistent purpose is what typifies the Orwellian image of the state. Thus, the senior servant of the state, O'Brien, says,

"The Party seeks power entirely for its own sake. We are not interested in the good of others; we are interested solely in power... We know that no one ever seizes power with the intention of relinquishing it. Power is not a means, but an end."[8]

The party is a unified agent of power coterminous with the state bureaucracy. Itself a hierarchy, only its élite (the Inner Party) has real power. Opposed to any human being having purposes other than those determined by itself, the élite seeks to ensure that everybody — but particularly those who administer its wishes, the lesser bureaucrats like Winston Smith himself — be its enthusiastic slaves. It is to make Winston fit this stereotype that he is taken to prison and reformed. As O'Brien tells him:

"We shall crush you down to the point from which there is no coming back... Never again will you be capable of ordinary human feeling. Everything will be dead inside you. Never again will you be capable of love, or friendship, or joy of living, or laughter, or curiosity, or courage, or integrity. You will be hollow. We shall squeeze you empty, and then we shall fill you up with ourselves."[9]

And there is never any doubt that the state will be successful. In his rebellion against the state Winston Smith lived in constant fear, always feeling that he would be caught. He is heroic in a pathetic sort of way, battling impossible odds, doomed from the start. *1984* becomes a tragedy in the classical sense of the term, with an individual fighting for personal significance against superhuman forces. That is the logical end of the ideology of the modern state, and it is against that which Orwell is warning us in novel form.

III

Orwell was not being prophetic, and the world of which he wrote is not inevitable. However, we are given a possibility, given the development of factors which he himself saw in his own time. So we must ask ourselves, "What aspects of our own society seem to fit the Orwellian pattern outlined in *1984?*" How does the state impinge upon our lives and consciences today in our "liberal democracies"? — in answer to which my discussion will refer principally to aspects of the contemporary Canadian state.

In approaching this question we should first remember that the largest group in Orwell's anti-utopia is the Proles, who make up the bulk of the population. Not involved in the administration of the state, this mass of the population is kept passively indifferent to questions of political power, although it is important to mobilize them through propaganda into a general support for state policies. Orwell gives us a Ministry of Truth whose purpose is the manipulation of the Proles into appropriate channels of belief and behaviour.

We do not have a Ministry of Truth, but the media does manipulate information. Chomsky and Herman have produced two volumes which show how the "free" American press follow the line of the State Department of the USA in reporting foreign events and policy. In Canada the disproportionate bulk of the press is equally selective and biased in its reporting, as Eleanor MacLean's excellent book, *Between the Lines,* reveals.[10] Friends and enemies are implicitly or explicitly identified, and praised and blamed accordingly.

At the same time, the bulk of the media is concerned with the trivial — with sports, gossip, popular entertainment and fashion. Then, beneath that, or with it, there is the never-ending supply of pulp publications and celluloid images — everything from Donald Duck to Harlequin Romances and snuff movies. The Pornography Section of Orwell's Ministry of Truth performed the same function as our own free market garbage. It directed the population's thought away from an assessment of the character of the world around them, debasing and destroying self-esteem. It was all part of the calculated depoliticization of the masses, which is the necessary condition of unchallenged rule. More an aspect of capitalism in our own society, it nonetheless continues to work to produce the same results.

With the bulk of the population accepting the prevailing political myths, minimally participating when it bothers to vote, largely indifferent, then those who play the political game are left largely to themselves. Looking at federal MPs, we note that they are rather less Spartan in their conditions than Orwell's party people as they use their positions to line their pockets. Most typical of the Canadian parliamentary system is not, however, the member of the elected House of Commons. At least those characters are expected to appear to cast their vote when the bells ring. Then like Pavlov's dogs they earn their $70,000-plus per annum by voting the way they are told to by the party whips. Nice work if you can get it, but hardly conducive to a critical posture by these voting machines who, in their activity, deny the autonomy of both themselves and the people whom they are supposed to represent. More typical even than the MP is the Canadian Senator, a party hack appointed according to a well-established system of patronage, and receiving $61,425 in 1984 if he or she can muster the energy to attend for a couple of days during each parliamentary session.[11]

Then, behind the public politics of party conformity, there are the bureaucrats, paid by the parties or by the public purse, who never come under the public gaze. The unelected officials, the professionals who despise the elected amateurs, protect their isolation. Under the pretence of political neutrality (although, indeed, they are largely neutral between the Tweedledums and

Tweedledees of our party system), the handmaidens of the perpetuation of the state organize themselves. They are the civil service, ranked and arranged under the deputy ministers as a self-perpetuating structure of political and social control. Winston Smith would have been quite at home there after his cure.

However, our own personal 1984 is not entirely subtle, not entirely dependent upon techniques of persuasion, be they media manipulation or the circus of politics. Any person raising a critical voice, suggesting that our democracy is an ineffective and immoral façade, becomes a target for the Security Branch of the RCMP. Consequently, even in the political gamesmanship which passes for sober discussion in Parliament (largely ignored by the public to the relief of the participants) the tip of the coercive iceberg of repression sometimes emerges. So we know that the security branch of the RCMP got 20% of the force's total budget in 1983 — as was revealed in an administrative bulletin, and reported to the House of Commons by NDP MP Svend Robinson in September 1983. And we know that the RCMP ran security checks on 76,521 public servants in 1982 — as Human Rights Commissioner Gordon Fairweather informed the Senate committee examining national security legislation in October, 1983. These were just procedural checks, to make sure that the civil servants in question were not closet communists, hawking secrets to the Russians. At a more sinister level the Security Service has taken upon itself the task of identifying and disrupting the existence of political targets selected by itself, in accordance with the fine political sense which we all know to be there in the average policeman's mind.

In April, 1980, the McDonald Commission gave specific information concerning ways in which the RCMP had pursued its political goal of spying upon, harassing, and stealing documents from extra-parliamentary targets with, literally, unwarranted zeal. In breaking the law they thus denied the very rule of law which is their *raison d'être*, making themselves the self-appointed protectors of the nation's political morality. They took to themselves the role of Orwellian Thought Police. In January 1984 information was still appearing from the Commission's enquiries. The police had filed false tax returns for a Canadian radical, in order "to disrupt the individual by exposing him to an income tax investigation (and to the possible expense of attaining legal and accounting assistance)..."[12] Typically, some information was withheld for "national security reasons."

A paranoid statist mentality persists in the RCMP Security Service. They have recruited participants to inform on the activities of persons supporting the El Salvador revolutionaries, persons organizing against racism, and those involved in the peace movement.[13] They have raided the Toronto offices of the Cruise Missile Conversion Project, seized documents and lists of names, and tapped the phones of activists.[14] Some have claimed that in the Vancouver area alone more than 3,700 telephone lines are under continuous wiretaps.[15]

Nearly all of this information, and it is by no means comprehensive, has appeared in the press. Does this not indicate a protection provided by the media against Orwellian conclusions? Hardly. It is merely evidence of ongoing police surveillance, and we have no idea what else goes on under the veil of national security. Moreover, it is absolutely justified by many members of the system, particularly by Robert Kaplan, the Solicitor-General of Canada at the time of writing. Also, this kind of information is essentially transitory. It is sometimes said that trying to understand political events by reading the news is like trying to tell the time by looking at the second hand of a clock. We see bits of information, which relate to the lives of very few, and which are rapidly forgotten. Grains of significant information are lost in the chaff of trivia.

The policing of the Canadian population, therefore, continues. On February 25, 1984, we were told that "the Government wants to make it easier for 17 of its investigative agencies to conceal their activities when they obtain information about people from the files of other federal departments and agencies."[16] This was an aspect of a proposed reform to the Privacy Act. Moreover, it seems highly probable that a new Security Intelligence Service will be created, with the specific task of acting as a political watchdog over "suspicious" elements at large in Canadian society. This new service is to be separate from the RCMP, whose bumbling incompetence had been revealed by the McDonald Commission (i.e., they had been discovered). Some of us would prefer the RCMP to keep its security responsibilities for that very reason. Better incompetent fascists than the more efficient variety, is the argument. Meanwhile, the denial of a private sphere, sacrosanct against state interference, remains. It worries liberals who remember the warnings of John Stuart Mill's essay *On Liberty,* published more than a century ago. It threatens those to the left of mainstream politics, whose values lie outside the sphere of received opinion; for it forbodes the increasing capacity of the state to perfect its policemen role and intrinsically coercive character.

The justification of this police surveillance is inevitably couched in terms of an external enemy, as if a few activits and writers might overthrow the Canadian political system with the help of a foreign power. That non-communists might find it in themselves to oppose American imperialism, to support the revolutionaries in Nicaragua and El Salvador, to oppose the testing of nuclear delivery systems such as the Cruise missile (which is also an armament mechanism), to support the Canadian withdrawal from NATO, to oppose racism — such a possibility seems unlikely to the security-minded mentality. Such a mentality refuses to believe that most Canadian dissidents, loosely defined as those who deny the efficacy of the capitalist and parliamentary system, also find communist systems highly (even more) unattractive. They are not likely to be attracted towards Soviet, let alone Chinese, paradigms of perfection. Nevertheless, the assertion of a connection between domestic and foreign "threats," however unreal, is the standard argument used to justify the arbitrary power of the police.

Nor should we forget that those policemen who are involved in out-of-the-ordinary police work get a larger sense of self-esteem than the mere traffic cop. How much greater is the sense of self-importance when you're checking up on a question of state security? The need to believe in a global competition and a foreign threat is of high significance here as an aspect of promoting one's own status. The bigger the stakes, the more important the stake-out! So the political and police paranoids continue to promote the fiction. The fact that there is probably nothing of international importance in Canada to protect — although we can never know for certain, for "security reasons" — is not considered. Thereafter, the political police are to be permitted to break the law, and the presumed constitutional rights of those who are targeted are not worth anything.

The police everywhere is a frightening establishment. The paramilitary character of its organization in Canada further stresses an attitude of being separate from the rest of the population. It also encourages an authoritarian mentality, a willingness to accept orders without question. The end product is that the police come to regard themselves as persons and as a hierarchy with the authority and responsibility to protect us from ourselves. Like all bureaucrats they come to regard the public, whom they are purportedly serving, as opponents. But for policemen, the public are also all potential criminals, and they are the watchdogs. With this splendidly Platonic conception (if they did but know it), regarding themselves as persons who see the world more clearly than ordinary folk, they take the right to impose upon us.

In so mundane a matter as the consumption of alcohol and driving a car, they use the excuse of alcohol-related accidents to stop anyone and everyone at will. Thus, although 33,050 cars were stopped in Vancouver in December 1983 only 115 people were charged. In Winnipeg the respective numbers were 8,561 and 58. These figures suggest that harassment of the public is more important than ensuring safety on the highways, which would involve a far more selective and judgemental intervention.[17]

Harassment and intimidation is the police style. If you are young and driving an old car, and therefore probably working class, you will be stopped and searched. If you have open liquor or a marijuana joint, you are charged and acquire a criminal record. You become an immediate suspect for later petty crimes and, in the event of another minor offence, you can end up doing time. You are sent to the best school for criminality — the prison. Thereby, you become criminalized by the police system, one purpose of which is the reproductin of the group in society which justifies its existence. In this process, as all lawyers know, the police lie persistently when on the witness stand in court. Only rarely do we find a judge taking the position of Judge Paul Matlow who, in May 1984, accused the police of incompetence and downright lying in the case before him; and accepted a defendant's claim that he had been viciously assaulted by a Metro Toronto police officer (rather than vice-versa).[18]

Consequently, we should see the harassment of political targets not as something unique, but as an extension of normal police practice. Violence is a feature of the process. So we should not be surprised that in May 1984, "a lawyer who alleged his 'throat was squeezed and wrist twisted' by RCMP officers when he refused to become a paid informer in 1972 has accepted a $23,000 out-of-court settlement from the federal Government."[19] Nor should we be less surprised that, "in November, 1982, RCMP Inspector Bernard Blier pleaded guilty to forcibly detaining Mr. Chamard (the lawyer in question) and was given an absolute discharge. A month later, Constable Richard Daigle was acquitted of kidnapping and holding the lawyer against his will."[20] The police state protects its own under the façade of the rule of law.

Intimidation, however, need not resort to strongarm tactics. In April of 1984 numerous activists in the peace movement in Canada received letters informing them that their mail and phone calls were being intercepted. No reason was given. In a letter which I saw, but did not personally receive, an indecipherable signature rode over the title (no name) of the Attorney General of Québec. It was a model of bureaucratic impersonalness, the nameless authority of the state, Big Brother watching over you. What should one do? Censor one's thoughts and withdraw from the peace movement. Worry always about what one says and does, no matter how legal the activity? Hesitate to exercise those rights supposedly guaranteed in writing? As another recipient has publicly said about his own letter: "What does that mean? That peace activists are considered criminal? That their activities have some way been criminalized? Is this a sign of things to come? That's the kind of thing that we are concerned about."[21] That is also the kind of thing that Orwell was concerned about, as should we all.

IV

None of this discussion leads on to the conclusion that our 1984 is a mirror image of the situation described by Orwell. However, the factors stressed by Orwell as primary to the degrading system which he conjured up for us do, quite obviously, still exist. At the very least we live in a partial Oceania. It can be said to be only partial because the arbitrary powers of the police in its controlling capacity are sometimes revealed and controlled; and there are sources of opposition to prevailing cultural prejudices in the form of radical publications and the activity of extra-par-

liamentary oppositions (such as the peace movement).
Yet even in the public revelation of police extremes, and even in the public character of political criticism, there remains the underlying evidence that:
1) The political orientation, capacity and actual repressive conduct of the police is widespread in our society, and
2) The political culture of our society, on the whole, is one which accepts the legitimacy of the *status quo,* and the authority of the police as protectors of the state.

In consequence, the critic of the system is faced with a significant ideological and organizational inhibition. He or she seems doomed to remain in a small minority. Specific issues, such as the threat of a nuclear holocaust, may bring out crowds of hundreds of thousands. However, at the end of the day, a view of *policy questions as being of only secondary importance to a thorough overhaul of the structures of power,* is held by few. For most members of a political demonstration, their action is seen as no more than a modern equivalent of a humble and faithful petition to their sovereign. The need for state power, expressed through a police and political hierarchy, is not questioned.

So all-pervasive is the authoritarian myth that those who are paid to think, the intellectuals, partake both innocently and enthusiastically in the process of state promotion. As Orwell himself speculated,

"... by the fourth decade of the twentieth century all the main currents of political thought were authoritarian. The earthly paradise had been discredited at exactly the moment when it became realizable. Every new Political theory, by whatever name it called itself, led back to hierarchy and regimentation."[22]

Belief and argument in favour of the inevitability of authority is indeed the common characteristic of everyone but the anarchists today. (Consequently, the anarchists are viewed by both communists and capitalists alike as either dangerous terrorists or crazy dreamers.) In communist-ruled states the Marxist "dictatorship of the proletariat" became party rule. The communist party replaced the proletariat in the creation of what Milovan Djilas called a "new class." That Leninist-Stalinist theory and practice of a "vanguard party" has persisted down to the present. Before his death the grand old Soviet ideologue, Mikhail Suslov, affirmed that even though the state may wither away, the party would persist. Then, in contrast to the frozen formulae of that statist ideology, social science in the West has been hypnotized by Michels' arguments concerning the "inevitability of oligarchy." However much our political scientists talk of interest groups and elections, political parties and electoral competitions, politics as the wielding of power by the few over the many is presumed.

If, however, this cultural and intellectual acceptance of authoritarianism is so general, why the enthusiastic attack upon radicals who form such an insignificant minority within the system? The horns of oppression may be occasionally visible above the fog of liberal democratic conceit, but they are seen by so few that it would seem to be unnecessary to stifle the voices of those who point towards them. Few listen to radicals, and few look at that to which they point.

As I have already suggested, an answer to this question may be found in the fact that "security" activity gives the police a greater sense of status. Link that targeting of internal dissidents with an external enemy and such activity becomes a justification for the arbitrary power of the police, and for the structure of the state itself. In addition, and as part of this process, although the North American dissident is but a minor aspect of the system overall, radicalism is invariably associated with violence. This is entirely wrong, but is asserted as a form of wish-fulfillment. If the radicals are violent, the argument goes, then all means of attack are permissible. Thus, when a bomb is exploded by a group of self-styled anarchists — as happened in Ontario at the Litton plant involved in production of missile parts a couple of years ago — every kind of broad response is permitted. Any organization or group associated with them in even the most remote way is open to the standard procedures of harassment. It does not require the application of the War Measures Act for Canadians to lose their civil rights. It's happening to some of us all the time because of the fertile imaginations of the hysterical and authoritarian personalities of those whose task it is to "protect" us. Extremism in the defence of liberty, as Barry Goldwater said in 1964, is permissible. Thereby the terrorism of the state takes upon itself a halo of legitimacy.

Looking again at Orwell's *1984* we see that Winston Smith swore an oath which committed him to any and every kind of violence, in strict obedience to revolutionary leaders whom he had never met, in pursuit of the destruction of the authoritarian state. On the other hand we should also note that all that Winston actually did was to make love to a woman (in opposition to established rules) and to think that the system was wrong. His thoughts were: "Not merely the love of one person but the animal instinct, the simple undifferentiated desire: that was the force that would tear the Party to pieces.... Their embrace had been a battle, the climax a victory. It was a blow struck against the Party. It was a political act."[23] Individual acts of terror had no part in the actuality of his personal rebellion against Big Brother.

The terrorist, the black-cloaked figure with a hidden bomb, is the popular image of the anarchist — and some who have called themselves anarchists have taken that route. However, like the tragic hero of *1984,* the anarchist is more likely to say, "If there is home... it lies in the proles."[24] The proles are, of course, the

165

proletariat, the dispossessed, everyone in society outside the hierarchy of political and economic power in Oceania. In a word, it is the masses; and Orwell's character was placing hope, as slim as it might appear, in a mass movement which seemed most unlikely to occur. This is sensible, for the killing of symbolic individuals does not alter the structures of power, and rather than raising public consciousness tends to turn public opinion against the radical perpetrators. Moreover, terror implies a moral absolutism which is most untypical of anarchists. To use terror is to take upon oneself the belief that one partakes of a higher truth than that seen by average mortals, to express in action a right which transcends the concerns of ordinary mortals. Terror dehumanizes, making persons into killable objects.

Terrorists excuse themselves by reference to a higher law — and that law is today most usually framed in nationalist terms, be it the terrorism of an FLQ or the militaristic response of the state to it. This is not anarchist, which position is usually stated thus:

"National terrorists oppose one nation with another. They consider their nation is at war with another nation. It is purely a matter of which side you're on as to whether the French Resistance is called 'terrorist' (the Germans called it such, the Allies didn't). Precisely the same reasoning applies to the Irish or the Arabs. They are indiscriminate in their attacks because they are nationalist — as long as they 'hit the enemy' it does not matter to them what their position in society is. They differ from the national armies, such as the British, French, German, Russian, American, only in status. The difference is not moral but legal... Nobody can, from a libertarian standard, defend nationalist attacks any more than war..."[25]

Consequently, there are practical, moral and ideological objections to the most usual form of terrorism in the modern world.

The anarchist's hope, like Orwell's, lies in a spontaneous mass movement of opposition. This has always been the source of effective attack upon state structures, in opposition to and in spite of the propaganda and the coercive capacity of specific systems. What happened in Hungary in 1956, in France and Czechoslovakia in 1968, in Poland in 1980, what is happening in Argentina and Chile and El Salvador today, what many in the peace movements of Germany and Britain and Canada and the USA are expressing in demonstrations and civil disobedience — all of these are examples of the inability of the modern state to persuade and/or command obedience in the face of fundamental opposition to its orders and policies. Speaking of the possibility of effective rebellion in even the most authoritarian systems, Martin Glaberman argued

"How do you revolt in a situation like that?... If you stop to think about it, it's impossible. The one advantage workers have is that they haven't the time to think about it. They have a resistance that they have to conduct every day of their lives. And if that resistance stopped, then the spontaneous outbreaks are impossible. What I'm talking about is the day-to-day resistance of the working class. Every day on the job you are trying to give your employer a little less, you're trying to protect yourself from the discipline which is routine, you're trying to protect your humanity when it is being demeaned by the way you are being treated... It is because that is continuous that these larger outbreaks take place."[26]

Broad apathy towards the political system and the workplace persist under both communist and capitalist regimes. In the last analysis, rebellion is possible because the state fails in persuading the citizens to support either itself or its laws. Social control through propaganda and ideological conditioning is not sufficient, and we can see it all the time.

When a Canadian soldier decided to shoot up the Québec National Assembly in May 1984 it was the brutal and cruel act of a mentally-disturbed young man. In political terms it was an irrelevant act, and would have remained so even if he had succeeded in assassinating members of the provincial assembly and government (as he had intended). As it was, he opened fire on a number of office employees, killing and injuring them. Any civilized person must condemn such actions — and most anarchists would combine this with a sigh of relief that it was a soldier, and not some self-styled radical civilian, who perpetrated the act, knowing how the police would have responded in that event. What is of interest here, however, is not the event itself, but the response of the public to it. Most people with whom newspaper reporters spoke saw fit to express regret that ordinary workers rather than politicians were the ones to suffer.[27] I suggest that this rather unkind response is yet another example of the ongoing antipathy of the public to state power, symbolized in the persons of its own elected politicians.

Popular antipathy towards authority and its symbols, activated, is the principal precondition which lies at the core of all the crises of political (and other) hierarchies. States have never collapsed because of the intrigues of small groups of self-styled leaders, who seek only to lead popular rebellions which are not of their making. Of course, this popular energy has been tapped and used by statists from every point in the political spectrum, and the carnival of revolution, that local autonomy and spontaneous rejection of imposed authority, has had to succumb to new generations of moral absolutists and political authoritarians. Each and every system of state authority has thereby remained oppressive, no matter what its ideological guise. Given those characteristics of the modern state which were emphasized by Orwell, and which we can see around us today, it is not difficult to view the contemporary alternatives. Either one thinks and acts independently of the state in perpetual scepticism and distrust of all structures of authority, or one contributes to those patterns of authority. Winston Smith was not given such a choice in Orwell's novel. We must make the choice before it also becomes impossible for us too.

NOTES

[1] Dwight MacDonald, "The Responsibility of Peoples," in *Politics*, Vol. 2, no. 3 (March 1945), p. 90. This journal was published in New York.
[2] *Ibid*, p. 91.
[3] *Ibid.*, p. 90.
[4] George Orwell, *1984*, p. 196. Penguin Books, 1984.
[5] *Ibid.*, p. 209.
[6] *The HAPOTOC Rebel*, September-December, 1977. Published in Amsterdam by the Help A Prisoner, Outlaw Torture Organizing Collective.
[7] Orwell, *op. cit.*, 161.
[8] *Ibid.*, p. 227.
[9] *Ibid.*, p. 270.
[10] In this paragraph reference is being made to the two volumes by Noam Chomsky and Edward S., Herman jointly called *The Political Economy of Human Rights*. Volume I is entitled *The Washington Connection and Third World Fascism;* Volume II is *After the Cataclysm: Post-war Indo-China and the Reconstruction of Imperial Ideology*. Both were published by Black Rose Books, Montréal, 1979. Eleanor MacLean's book, *Between the Lines: How to Detect Bias and Propaganda in the News and Everyday Life,* was published by Black Rose Books in 1981.
[11] Figures published in *The Globe and Mail*, December 30, 1983.
[12] *The Globe and Mail*, January 31, 1984.

[13] The *Ottawa Citizen,* June 30, 1983.
[14] *The Globe and Mail,* April 13, 1983.
[15] This figure was provided in *Newsletter Number One* (February, 1984) by the Citizens Against State Surveillance group in Montreal.
[16] Report by Jeff Salot in *The Globe and Mail,* February 25, 1984).
[17] Report by Michael Tenszen, *The Globe and Mail,* December 30, 1983.
[18] *The Globe and Mail,* May 3, 1984.
[19] *The Globe and Mail,* May 4, 1984.
[20] *Ibid.*
[21] Statement by Norman Nawrocki, a Montréal freelance writer and public relations adviser to a Montréal peace group. See *The Globe and Mail,* May 2, 1984.
[22] Orwell, *op. cit.,* 177.
[23] *Ibid.,* p. 112.
[24] *Ibid.,* p. 64.
[25] *Black Flag* (United Kingdom), December 1976, Vol. IV, no. 12.
[26] Martin Glaberman, "Poland and Eastern Europe," presented at the third annual conference on Human Rights, January 23, 1983, Kingston, Ontario. See *Speaking Out.* Vol. 2, no. 3-4.
[27] On May 8, 1984, Cpl. Denis Lortie of the Canadian armed forces killed 3 people and wounded another 13 workers in the Québec National Assembly. The following report was written by Graham Fraser in *The Globe and Mail* on May 12, 1984; "Emerging from the funeral of the three victims of Tuesday's shooting in the Québec National Assembly, politicians from both sides of the House were unnerved by the reactions they had heard last week. "People are going so far as to say, 'It's a shame those poor innocent people were killed instead of some nasty politicians,'" said a visibly shaken Guy Tardif, Housing and Consumer Protection Minister...."I heard that in my riding," said Pierre Paradis, Liberal MNA for Brome-Missisquoi. "People are saying, 'What a shame it was honest citizens instead of politicians.' It wasn't just anglophones, either — francophones too."

Authoritarian Education

by Robert S. Mayo

Compulsory education rests upon a remarkable congeries of compromises and assumptions, one of the most important of which is surely the widespread belief that the need for all young people to spend the best part of many years in school is so well established and manifestly justified that it warrants no further discussion. It has hardly even been necessary for members of the educational establishment to vilify and pillory advocates of deschooling, for whenever and wherever their message has been broadcast it has generally been accorded scant sympathy or attention. This reluctance to contemplate the possibility that the whole enterprise is inherently flawed and doomed to fail is rather puzzling when one considers the regularity with which a hullaballoo is raised, in those countries where the system is most securely entrenched, about the unsatisfactory performance of the schools. Nowhere is this situation more baffling than in North America.

Within the past two or three years yet another crisis has been perceived or manufactured, with particular emphasis being placed upon declining test scores at various levels. Sundry task forces and commissions were set up to investigate the matter, and in due course conclusions and recommendations came forth: everyone must try harder. More tests, mandated state requirements, more homework, longer school hours, stricter discipline, more stringent training and certification of teachers, with more vigilant quality control — all these and more are on the agenda.[1] Indeed, some attempts have already been made to implement some of these measures. In Québec, for example, where the ministry of education enjoys pretty comprehensive control of the whole system, longer school hours, with a supposedly tightened curriculum, were introduced during the 1983-84 school year, with results which were quite as dismal as had been anticipated by the teachers' unions when negotiations had been abruptly terminated by the government the previous year, and conditions of work had been arbitrarily decreed by the government with draconian force.

Naturally many voices of reason have been raised to decry this general tendency to get tough in the schools, but their ideas do not appear likely to prevail. In keeping with the political tenor of the times, failed policies must be tried again with redoubled effort. The educational and social philosophy which is embodied in this programme of striving for excellence has been exposed with admirable clarity and simplicity by one of the most estimable and persistent critics of coercive education. John Holt identifies three metaphors which, he claims, determine what most teachers do in school.

"The first of these metaphors presents education as an assembly line in a bottling plant or canning factory. Down the conveyor belts come rows of empty containers of sundry shapes and sizes. Beside the belts is an array of pouring and squirting devices, controlled by employees of the factory. As the containers go by, these workers squirt various amounts of different substances — reading, spelling, math, history, science — into the containers.

Upstairs, management decides when the containers should be put on the belt, how long they should be left on, what kinds of materials should be poured or squirted into them at what times, and what should be done about containers whose openings (like pop bottles) seem to be smaller than the others, or that seem to have no openings at all."[2]

The second metaphor likens students in school to laboratory rats, which are presented with ridiculous un-ratlike tasks to perform, with attendant rewards and punishments for positive or negative reinforcement. The third metaphor, which Holt considers to be, perhaps, the most destructive and dangerous of all, follows from the first pair and refers to the role of the school as a mental hospital or treatment centre. The awkward squad, those individuals who are not filled on the assembly line, or who cannot or will not perform the allotted tasks in the cage must be defective, and their 'learning disabilities' must be diagnosed and cured. Holt is not optimistic about the chances of educators recognizing how false and misleading are these metaphors which dominate their system and renouncing them.

The decisions which are taken by Holt's management upstairs are, of course, all too often narrow-minded and arbitrary. One has only to look, for example, at the way in which the typical school system, backed by a comprehensive examination and certification process, concentrates upon linguistic and logical-mathematical abilities. Recently the psychologist Howard Gardner has identified seven different kinds of intelligence; in addition to the two favourites of schoolmonks, which have just been mentioned, there are said to be five other kinds of intelligence, which Gardner considers to be every bit as important: spatial, musical, bodily-kinesthetic, and two forms of personal intelligence — interpersonal, knowing how to deal with others, and intrapersonal, knowledge of self. There is no obvious reason why any of these should be given priority over the others by any educational system.[3]

In fact, it does not really matter whether there are actually five, or more, distinct kinds of intelligence; the point is that almost every school neglects the development of important human qualities and abilities. A.S. Neill used to complain about the exclusive focus upon the part above the neck, but even that was probably far too sanguine a view of the matter. Most schools neglect a considerable part of what lies between the ears, in order to concentrate upon what is apparently considered to be their strong suit, the nurturing of linguistic and logical-mathematical abilities. Of course it is possible that this common reluctance on the part of educational authorities to meddle with other human capacities, even while they do occasionally pay lip service to at least some of them, is due to genuine modesty — a widespread recognition of the futility of introducing sundry important human endeavours into the compulsory school curriculum.

Many influential people in the field of education are doubtless aware of the existence of such works as Ashley Montagu's *Learning Non-Aggression,* a collection of essays which recount the various ways in which children in seven different non-literate societies are raised to live with a minimum of aggressive behaviour. Even though these educators may recognize the immense value of developing such interpersonal intelligence, of greater worth, perhaps, than anything which is currently included in the standard North American curriculum, they do not rush to incorporate such items into their scheme of education. In order to do so they would have to extend their authority and envelop infants in their grasp, a desideratum which applies to most forms of social conditioning. The educational pundits display a certain ambivalence on this point, insisting on the one hand upon the importance of starting early, especially if there is any reason to suspect some kind of disadvantage in the child's home background, yet wishing to restrict such early intervention to solid, cognitive material. The latter tendency has recently been most clearly expressed in Diane Ravitch's *The Troubled Crusade: American Education, 1945-1980.*

Such reticence on the part of at least some educators may be due to concern about legitimate parental rights rather than any sense of guilt about grabbing the little beggars and doing unto them before they know what has hit them. A majority amongst educators might well assent to the proposition that the true goal of education is the production of autonomous individuals, but how many would demur at the corollary, that this might imply a minimum of interference and intervention in the lives of those individuals? Others may merely be deterred by a temporary lack of confidence in the efficacy of early intervention; nothing is inherently off limits and safe from pruning, modification or forced growth.

We are assured, for example, by Carolyn Zahn-Wexler of the U.S. National Institute of Mental Health that the development of emotions is really an unexplored area, but now psychologists are developing a detailed theory of how empathy is triggered and are identifying the forces that bring out or stifle a child's altruism[4]. I am reminded of Paul Goodman's suggestion that if the job of teaching children how to speak were to be entrusted to professional educators we would all be stammerers and stutterers.

Although up until now the alarms and commotion about declining educational standards have been mainly focused upon the inadequate performance of primary, and especially secondary schools, it appears highly likely that attention will be shifted to what are now called the pre-school years. The reason for this shift was quite simply explained by Howard Gardner in a recent interview: "I would assess intellectual propensities from an early age. I use the word *propensities* because I don't believe intelligences are fixed for many years. The earlier a strength is discovered, the more flexibility there is to develop it. Similarly, if a child has a low propensity, the earlier intervention begins, the easier it is to shore up the child. So early diagnosis is important."[5] Of course this begs the question, as Gardner himself admits; will it be strenuous exploitation of a talent early revealed, or urgent remedial action for some latent weakness? Who, indeed, will decide what action will be taken? A concatenation of circumstance leads to the almost inevitable conclusion that those people who presently wield authority in the educational domain will absorb this new territory with comparative ease.

A burgeoning demand for daycare facilities and a prolonged recession in the education business, with sharply decreased enrollment and dismal demographic prospects, will surely provide more than enough stimulus to sustain this partial take-over of infancy. It will not be hard to put a good face on it; in terms of John Holt's third metaphor early diagnosis is to be most fervently desired. Beyond that, Gardner refers to the Suzuki method of teaching music; "This method creates an environment that is rich with music; mothers play with the youngsters for 2 hours a day from the time they reach age 2. Within a few years, all participants become decent musicians." He goes on to say that, "in theory, we could 'Suzuki' everything. The more time and energy invested early in life on a particular intelligence, the more you can buoy it up. I am not advocating this approach, merely pointing out the possibilities."[6] One can easily imagine how, with suitable public relations efforts and support from various interested educational experts, resistance from a hitherto wary body politic might be overcome.

Parents have presumably been observing their offspring with varying degrees of sympathy and discernment since time immemorial, just as they and their kin normally took care of education before the advent of formal mass schooling. The argument to the effect that such observation should now be carried forward on a scientific basis is all too plausible. Those who wish to proceed with such a policy, and who also profess a belief in the importance of human rights display a remarkable insensitivity to the rights of young persons. Naturally safeguards would be put in place, and the utmost of professional care would be lavished upon the whole process, yet nagging doubts about the propriety of such an invasion of privacy cannot be so easily allayed.

This is not to suggest, however, that the efficacy of early intervention can be taken for granted, and that it is merely the morality of it all which remains in question. A number of psychologists and researchers, including some highly respected figures, have cast doubt upon the expediency of the whole enterprise. Prof. Sandra Scarr, president of the Behavior Genetics Association and editor of the journal *Developmental Psychology,* declares:

"The sort of behavior we can measure in infancy doesn't predict later intellectual development, neither mild retardation nor precociousness. Mental and motor tests during the first year of life don't tell us anything about later development, except for organically damaged babies or those so retarded that they score below 90 percent of other babies on the test. Infant intelligence is so different from later intelligence that you can't predict from one to the other. In fact, all babies who are not defective reach the same level of infant intelligence. Some just reach it faster than others."[7]

Of course Prof. Scarr may be talking about a more limited range of intelligences than Prof. Gardner, but it is one principle which is in dispute. Although Scarr emphasizes the importance of genetic and hereditary factors, she also alludes to the responsibility of parents to help their children become the most they can with what they've got.

Most parents do not need any psychologist to make them aware of this responsibility; presumably this moral obligation plays no small part in sustaining the whole compulsory school system, however unsatisfactory, uneven and unfair the results may be. Yet there are clearly other, ultimately much more powerful reasons, why the coercive apparatus of schooling has been kept in place, and has grown, both in extent and in the depth of the impact upon young lives. The laws which were enacted to establish the first system of compulsory education in the English-speaking world in the Massachussetts Bay colony in June 1642 reveal a lack of confidence on the part of wise leaders in the ability or diligence of the populace in fulfilling their obligations in this respect.

"For as much as the good education of children is of singular behoof and benefit to any commonwealth, and whereas many parents and masters are too indulgent and negligent of their duty of that kind, it is ordered that the selectmen of every town ... shall have a vigilant eye over their neighbors, to see first that none of them shall suffer so much barbarism in any of their families, as not to endeavour to teach, by themselves or others, their children and apprentices..."[8]

In his account of the development of compulsory education in the United States, Murray Rothbard exposes the profound mistrust, which the so-called fathers of the public school system in various states felt, and sometimes even openly expressed, regarding parents and children. It is rather ironic that *Newsweek* magazine in its cover story on "Saving Our Schools", May 9, 1983, should have singled out North Carolina as the state to lead the way back to quality education; "North Carolinians seem determined not only to make their schools do the job they were created to do but also to show the rest of the country that excellence in public education is not only possible, but entirely necessary." It just happens that Archibald D. Murphey, the most influential figure in the establishment of the public school system in North Carolina was, as Rothbard points out, unusually explicit in describing what those schools were created to do:

"In these schools the precepts of morality and religion should be inculcated, and habits of subordination and obedience be formed... Their parents know not how to instruct them... The state, in the warmth of her affection and solicitude for their welfare, must take charge of those children, and place them in school where their minds can be enlightened and their hearts can be trained to virtue."[9]

However much latter day authoritarians may agree with these sentiments, they would surely have to be couched in more diplomatic terms. Indeed, there is a parallel recurring theme in the justification for compulsory public education, which tends towards the same goal whilst being altogether more palatable to those who harbour democratic pretensions. Without having recourse to the wisdom of the ancient Greeks, one can trace a steady tradition back to the 18th century, according to which it is impossible to have a genuine democracy if you do not have universal education with a certain common core curriculum. This argument has resurfaced in full vigour in the latest spate of crisis literature; it is a central premise of Diane Ravitch's book and it is the very foundation stone of Mortimer J. Adler's educational manifesto, *The Paideia Proposal.* "The two — universal suffrage and universal schooling — are inextricably bound together. The one without the other is a perilous delusion."[10] Adler lays out the requisite curriculum, which, he insists, can be covered by all students, in considerable detail.

This is where things begin to get rather tricky. Adler always speaks in terms which indicate that all of this apparatus is being set up for the benefit of individuals within the society, but many others have drifted over into the dangerous assumption that the state or the polity has interests of its own, foremost amongst which is a suitably (by its own definition) educated citizenry. Long before the totalitarians of the 20th century came along such a notion had taken firm root in the United States, just as in other places where one might more readily expect it. In 1830 Calvin Stowe, another eminent figure in the history of American education, declared: "A man has no more right to endanger the state by throwing upon it a family of ignorant and vicious children, than he has to give admission to the spies of an invading army."[11] One does not have to look far in order to find equivalent or even stronger statements in modern times.

Indeed, the logic of this position can be, and has been, carried much further, well beyond the boundaries which are normally recognized for the sphere of education. If one recognizes the need of the state, or to put it in slightly less stark terms, of society, to be continuously replenished with orderly, co-operative citizens, then one must look to the most effective means of ensuring the attainment of that desired end. Carried to the extreme, this might, of course, involve a programme of eugenics — unlikely perhaps, but not wildly far-fetched. Indeed, even though quality control has not yet, so far as I am aware, been adopted as state policy anywhere, control over the quantity of reproduction is already vigorously enforced in China and Rumania, with the purpose of restriction in the former case, and stimulation in the latter.

If one accepts the proposition that parents play a vital, predominantly determining role in the pre-school education of children, then one may well wish to focus more attention upon the competence of prospective parents to embark upon such an endeavour, which is fraught with such risks for themselves, the offspring, and the rest of society. Programmes of mandatory parenthood training and licensing have long since been advocated. For example, in 1973 Prof. Roger W. McIntire proposed a system of mandatory universal birth control, with permission to procreate only being granted to those who can furnish proof that they have followed a course of instruction in parenthood training and passed an examination in the subject. Even then he made so bold as to assert that "psychology and related sciences have by now established some child-rearing principles that should be part of every parent's knowledge."[12] The list of principles which McIntire adumbrates is heavily biased towards behaviour modification, which would be anathema to some critics, but, as McIntire explains it, "their revisions or additions to the list only strengthen my argument that our science has a great deal to teach that would be relevant to a parenthood-licensing program." It is doubtful that such confidence is widely shared outside the field of psychology, and even those people who approve in principle of parenthood training have ample reason to doubt that any reliable body of information is available which might justify such intervention now. In any case, the very possibility of yielding up such an important area of human activity to supposedly expert authorities is pretty disturbing.

Lest all of this should appear to be altogether conjectural and implausible, let me hasten to point out, as did McIntire himself, that screening procedures of a much more arbitrary kind have long been in place for a certain class of parents, namely those who adopt children. In Sweden the requirement was already established, by law, many years ago to report the birth of every child to the local child welfare centre, to be followed by a visit to the home by a representative to assess conditions and report findings to the doctors at the centres. In one year in the late sixties, in a nation of about eight million people, twenty-one thousand children were removed from the custody of their own parents.[13] The continuing concern about the incompetence of many parents was given voice recently by Prof. James Q. Wilson, especially insofar as parents' mistakes produce brats and delinquents. Wilson laments the fact that "the principal barrier to success in helping troubled families is that they resist help", but he "shudders at the thought of developing, as some politicians too eager for the national spotlight have proposed, a 'national family policy'."[14] Instead he advocates the incorporation of sensible parenting techniques in the school curriculum, using the most sophisticated means of persuasion available.

The burden which incompetent parents impose upon society in the form of delinquents, criminals and misfits, always assuming that it is indeed their fault, provides what is probably the most politically persuasive argument for entrusting greater powers of management and supervision to the state. Some years ago a certain Dr. Hutschnecker, who had allegedly treated Richard Nixon in connection with a distressing personal handicap back in the sixties, proposed the establishment of a network of compulsory summer camps for boys between the ages of six and eight. There the lads would be screened for criminal propensities, and those who would be deemed to pose a particular risk for society would be subjected to the ministrations of appropriate experts. Fortunately his proposal was extremely coolly received in most quarters, due, presumably in no small measure, to the overtly totalitarian methods which he envisaged in order to achieve his goal. The more obviously humanitarian and rational methods of influencing the ways in which children are raised, which have been advanced by Prof. Wilson, seem to me to enjoy much better prospects for being adopted.

It can be argued quite plausibly that all of this is being perpetrated with the best interests of the young person, as well as those of society, in mind. Nor is it hard to find examples of palpably distorted and cruel child-rearing practices. A recent article in the magazine *Free Inquiry* documents many horror stories involving child abuse amongst ultrafundamentalist sects.[15] Many governments which display remarkable solicitude concerning the proper education of children, down to the last minutiae, turn out to be amazingly lethargic in this respect. For example, during the past eight years the government of the province of Québec has zealously used the school system of the province to further its own language policy; ministers of education and their minions have ridden roughshod over the jurisdiction of local school boards in their determination to impose their will and set the youth of the province on the path to righteousness, with school curricula being re-ordered from top to bottom every which way. Yet all the while many cases of gross abuse were being brought to light with very little action being taken by the government. For example, for years serious questions have been raised about the controversial religious sect Apostles of Infinite Love at St. Jovite, with allegations, made publicly by former residents, of mistreatment and woefully inadequate education; yet the government apparently never bothered to exert pressure upon the local school commission to find out what was going on at this curious institution within their jurisdiction. Only after renewed public allegations and a minor public scandal did the school commission begin to move with glacial speed to look into the matter in April, 1984.[16]

I do not, however, rush to condemn the school commissioners for their apparently lackadaisical attitude. I merely refer to the manifest hypocrisy of governments in these matters. Beyond legitimate concern for the physical safety and well-being of children one has good reason to be circumspect about imposing any particular method of child-rearing which may be given an imprimatur by the current crop of childcare specialists. In the early seventies Prof. Jerome Kagan was already a highly respected expert in the field of early human development, who subscribed to the theories propounded by Freud, Piaget and sundry eminent learning theorists, according to which intelligence can be predicted during the first year or two of life and early learning deficiencies are presumed to be irreversible. Then he visited Guatemala and got a rude surprise: he spent some time observing the child-rearing practices of Indians in an ancient pre-Columbian village. As he describes it:

"I saw infants in the first years of their lives completely isolated in their homes, because parents believe that sun and dust and air or the gazes of either pregnant women or men fresh with perspiration from the field will cause illness. It's the evil-eye belief. So the infants are kept in the hut. Now these are bamboo huts, and there are no windows, so the light level in this hut at high noon in a perfectly azure sky is what it should be at dusk. Very dark. Although parents love their children — mothers nurse on demand and hold their infants close to their bodies — they don't talk or interact with them. And there are no toys. So at one and one-half years of age, you have a very retarded child."[17]

This all sounds pretty grim, and doubtless most childcare experts would today share Kagan's own initial reaction. "If I had seen infants like the Guatemalans in America prior to my experience, I would have gotten very upset, called the police, had the children removed, and begun to make gloomy statements about the fact that it was all over for these children." He goes on, however, to reveal a paradox; he found the 11-year-old children in the village to be gay, alert, active, and affective — just as much so as kids of a comparable age back home in the United States. Indeed, he even found the Guatemalan children "*more* impressive than Americans in a set of 'culture-fair' tests — where the words and the materials are familiar."

Mistrust in the ability of most parents to raise their children in a humane and intelligent manner is by no means restricted to the circle of narrow-minded authoritarians. It was A.S. Neill, one of the most libertarian of educators, who said "the first enemy of children is the ignorance of parents."[18] And again, "the problem is parental, always parental. Children are ruined by the complexes of their parents,"[19] he declared. In fact, he wanted to see the establishment of enough schools modelled after his own Summerhill so that every child could enjoy the benefits of boarding school. The problem, in his opinion, is that parents insist upon shaping their kids in their own image. "The first rule for parents should be: I shall not make my child in my own image. I am not good enough, wise enough to tell my child how to live."[20] Finally Neill came to the conclusion that he had been mistaken when he said that he didn't want to accept any new pupil over seven years old; he decided that he should modify that to seven months before birth. In *A Primer of Libertarian Education* Joel Spring discusses Neill's ideas about institutionalized child-rearing, and makes an interesting comparison with collective child rearing on an Israeli Kibbutz. At the very least, it is evident that North American society is not yet ready to provide acceptable alternatives to the nuclear family. As Spring commented, "It is a dreary prospect to think of public schools operating child-care centers. That would be the final triumph of the process of schooling."[21]

Thus one is left with some pretty hard choices to make. Does one leave children in the custody of parents, who are all too likely to be inadequately equipped and prepared for their task, or does one look for institutions such as Summerhill or the Kibbutz, where the children will truly be given free rein to develop from autonomous youngsters into autonomous adults? Will there be enough Neills around to ensure that the temptation to mould, to help, to intervene for their own good will be resisted? Ultimately it really is a question of trust. Extraordinarily strong nerves are required of anyone who has gone through the standard educational system and been conditioned to the prevailing value system, if she or he is going to take seriously the notion of young people being permitted to learn and discover the world in their own way at their own pace. Forbearance may amount to torture as one contemplates the possibility of a talent left undiscovered or undeveloped, or of a handicap which might be alleviated most effectively during those earliest, most formative years, if Gardner is to be believed. Can one really believe Neill when he says, "Given the choice of foods, self-regulated children will eat according to their individual physical needs?"[22]

The answer is, of course, that one must believe and one must trust, if one is to take at all seriously the beliefs about freedom which are so profusely intoned and invoked throughout our society. Naturally one cannot be sure that this society will be perpetuated; if young people or old feel the need to learn they will do so, as long as they are not hindered, but there are no guarantees in education any more than in any other area where true freedom is acquired and used. Sharp disagreement may remain over the point at which young people are ready to avail themselves of such opportunities; John Holt proposes that "the rights, privileges, duties, responsibilities of adult citizens be made *available* to any young person, of whatever age, who wants to make use of them."[23] The authors of *Education by Choice: The Case for Family Control,* on the other hand, are quite adamant in maintaining that autonomy can only come as the child approaches the teens. "Under no system — conventional or radical, schooled or deschooled — will a six-year old exercise control over his learning. His impotence is not the political or cultural artifact of a cruel society. It is the lack of strength and experience in the child. The notion of liberating small children is nonsense... little children will not be liberated; they will be dominated. The only question is by whom and for what ends."[24]

No doubt most people would agree with this latter assessment, but I do not see how it in any way invalidates Holt's views. In his book *Escape from Childhood* he provides numerous examples of the ways in which the freedom of young children is trampled upon in a totally unnecessary manner. Eventually the absurdity of the treatment of minors becomes palpable; I have often engaged in a discussion on political topics with a class of students half of whom are under the official age of majority, and half of whom are over it, and I have never yet been able to pick out the minors without checking the class list, which has the ages coded on it. Those who fear that young people will run amok as soon as they are given half an opportunity, and that they will reject all the values and institutions of the older generations, display incredibly damaging and insulting mistrust, as well as lack of confidence in the inherent quality of their own ways.

Unfortunately, for the foreseeable future, the sceptics are surely going to prevail. As Joel Spring pointed out, "the real disagreements, therefore, go beyond educational technique; they involve the very nature of social change. Theories of education are just one very important aspect of an overall theoretical perspective about how society should change."[25] Spring discerned two distinct basic models. According to the first of these the child is treated as an object to be worked upon and shaped for the good of society; in the second case the principal concern is with increasing individual autonomy. The plethora of reports and tough recommendations for educational excellence, and the manner in which they have been received during the past couple of years do not leave much room for optimism. It is, perhaps, a rather depressing measure of the times that even a critic such as Dr. Benjamin Spock should feel constrained to write, in response to this latest trend in an article entitled "Coercion in the Classroom Won't Work", "All high school students — even those firmly intending to study and work at computers or dress design — should be seduced, by inspired teaching methods, into studying the sciences and humanities that have a bearing on their chosen fields."[26]

So we come full circle; must we resign ourselves to an indefinite continuation, and perhaps even an extension downwards, of an authoritarian educational system? Perhaps so, but there is a glimmer of hope here and there amidst the gathering gloom. A remarkable assortment of critics, ranging all the way from Milton Friedman to Colin Ward and Paul Goodman, have advocated the introduction of some form of voucher system, in order to open the way for more variety, innovation, competition or freedom of choice in the field of education. This would involve the distribution by governments of vouchers worth a certain specified amount to parents; they could then present a voucher for each child to the educational institution of their choice, and the school would in turn collect the appropriate sum of money from the government. In some versions of this scheme schools would also be permitted to charge extra fees over and above the amount provided by the voucher, in order to provide a superior quality of education, and perhaps not coincidentally, to discourage a certain class of applicants. The idea of a voucher system has always been repugnant to most liberals, who fear that it would undermine and destroy the public education system. I believe that they are unduly pessimistic, and that many new and unexpected vistas may be opened up. It is quite conceivable that anxious politicians, intent upon reducing expenditures in the area of education, will take up this concept. I rejoice in the thought that the best laid schemes of mice and men gang aft agley, especially those of politicians, and hope that much good may come of any such new departures, despite the probability that any state would retain supervisory power over any institution which would be eligible for a voucher programme.

Even in the worst of times bits of good news trickle in; in March, 1982 the government of the province of Alberta gave serious thought to the idea of repealing the compulsory school attendance law. The minister of education declared that the law merited reconsideration and may not even be necessary. This brought an editorial reaction from the Montreal *Gazette* to the effect that "the government out there has gone slightly off its rocker."[27] Alas, there was no reason to panic so, as nothing came of it this time. In any case, the minister was probably right when he said, "Even if we did away with compulsory education, the vast majority of parents would still send their children to public schools." Nevertheless it would have been an encouraging gesture. Yet even as the martinets and grade-keepers of the established educational system proceed on their dreary way, there is much consolation to be derived from the thought that, despite years of cohibition, there are people out there imbued with a libertarian spirit. The truth is that no one has yet discovered a reliable recipe for producing good people; very few of the most free-thinking people whom I know enjoyed a Summerhillian experience during their schooldays. Who, for example, amongst such figures as Bakunin, Kropotkin, Proudhon, Goldman, Neill, Goodman, Orwell, or Holt escaped completely the bane of rigid schooling? I like to think of Kagan's unexpected discovery amongst those Guatemalan children; who knows what vipers the persistent pedagogues are clasping to their bosoms?

Unfortunately the corollary to this is the temptation, to which, alas, some honest libertarians have succumbed, to devise their own enlightened version of what was imposed upon them in their youth. If some of these schemes are implemented on a small scale they do little harm and much good; for all their limitations such institutions as Summerhill or the Children's Republic of Bemposta, Spain serve as valuable examples and sources of inspiration. Yet it should by now be clear that no blueprint exists, or is likely to exist, for educational perfection; uniformity in this area of life is inherently undesirable, and if something works well it is quite likely that more means worse rather than better. Variety is of the essence, and it is ironic indeed that those who believe most fervently in freedom might wish to foist their own interpretation of it upon all those who come after them; the road to hell may be paved with good intentions, be they libertarian or otherwise.

NOTES

[1] In the period 1982-4 ten blue-ribbon studies appeared in the United States alone.
Academic Preparation for College, Educational Equality Project; The College Board, New York, N.Y., 1983.
America's Competitive Challenge: The Need for a National Response, The Business-Higher Education Forum, Washington, D.C., 1983.
Educating Americans for the 21st Century, Commission on Pre-Collegiate Education in Math, Science and Technology; National Science Board, Washington, D.C., 1983.
High School: A Report on Secondary Education in America, Ernest L. Boyer; Carnegie Foundation for the Advancement of Teaching, Harper and Row, New York, N.Y., 1983.
Horace's Compromise: The Dilemma of the American High School, Theodore R. Sizer; National Association of Secondary School Principals and National Association of Independent Schools, Houghton Mifflin, Boston, 1984.
Making the Grade, Task Force on Federal Elementary and Secondary Education Policy; Twentieth Century Fund, New York, N.Y., 1983.
A Nation at Risk, National Commission on Excellence in Education; U.S. Department of Education, Washington, D.C., 1983.
The Paideia Proposal: An Educational Manifesto, Mortimer J. Adler; The Paideia Group, Macmillan, New York, N.Y., 1982.
A Place Called School, John J. Goodlad; Institute for the Development of Educational Activities, McGraw-Hill, New York, N.Y., 1983.
Successful Schools for Young Adolescents, Joan Lipsitz; National Institute of Education, Transaction Books, New Brunswick, N.J., 1983.
[2] John Holt, "Why Teachers Fail", *The Progressive,* Vol. 48, No. 4, April 1984, p. 32.

[3] Howard Gardner, *Frames of Mind: The Theory of Multiple Intelligences,* Basic Books, New York, N.Y., 1983.
[4] *Newsweek,* Vol. 103, No. 11, March 12, 1984, p. 76.
[5] *U.S. News & World Report,* Vol. 96, No. 11, March 19, 1984, p. 78.
[6] Ibid.
[7] "What's a Parent To Do?", PT Conversation with Sandra Scarr, *Psychology Today,* Vol. 18, No 5, May 1984, p. 60.
[8] Cited in Murray Rothbard, *For a New Liberty: The Libertarian Manifesto,* Collier Books, New York, N.Y., 1978, p. 123.
[9] Op. cit., p. 124.
[10] Mortimer J. Adler, *The Paideia Proposal: An Educational Manifesto,* Macmillan, New York, N.Y., 1982, p. 3.
[11] Murray Rothbard, op. cit., p. 125.
[12] Roger W. McIntire, "Parenthood Training or Mandatory Birth Control: Take Your Choice," *Psychology Today,* Vol. 7, No. 10, October 1973, p. 132.
[13] Roland Huntford, *The New Totalitarians,* Stein & Day, New York, N.Y., 1972.
[14] James Q. Wilson, "Raising Kids", *The Atlantic,* Vol. 252, No. 4, October 1983, p. 56.
[15] Lowell D. Streiker, "Ultrafundamentalist Sects and Child Abuse", *Free Inquiry,* Vol. 4, No. 2, Spring 1984, pp. 10-16.
[16] Montreal *Gazette,* May 1, 1984.
[17] "A Conversation with Jerome Kagan", Saturday Review of Education, Vol. 1, No. 3, March 10, 1973, p. 41.
[18] A.S. Neill, "Freedom Works", in *Children's Rights,* Panther Books, London, 1972, p. 139.
[19] Ibid., p. 140.
[20] Ibid., p. 146.
[21] Joel Spring, *A Primer of Libertarian Education,* Black Rose Books, Montreal, 1975, p. 124.
[22] A.S. Neill, op. cit., p. 147.
[23] John Holt, *Escape from Childhood,* Ballantine Books, New York, N.Y., 1975, p. 1.
[24] John E. Coons & Stephen D. Sugarman, *Education By Choice: The Case for Family Control,* University of California Press, Berkeley, 1978, pp. 23-4.
[25] Joel Spring, op. cit., pp. 129-30.
[26] Benjamin Spock, "Coercion in the Classroom Won't Work", *The Atlantic,* Vol. 253, No. 4, April 1984, p. 30.
[27] Montreal *Gazette,* March 22, 1982.

The Real Rocky Horror Picture Show: State and Politics in Contemporary Society

by Stephen Schecter

The State is dead, long live the State! The declaration holds to the world in bitter irony the deformed mirror of its own ambiguities. In a few, relatively restricted spheres, most people are well-fed, housed in something more than shanty-towns, and entertained by more stimuli than they can adequately handle. These are the areas where the State is most secure, and its citizens consequently somewhat insulated not only from the nasty, brutish and short existence of unbridled civil society but also from the harsh caprice of the modern prince. And yet, something still is rotten in the State of Denmark, while beyond its borders history itself seems to be going backwards.

One would have thought that Auschwitz marked a terminal point, but in vast parts of the world today practices developed by middle-Europa totalitarianism have become standard political procedure. For those dissidents which the Soviet Union has found too difficult to intern in psychiatric hospitals or labour camps the Communist Party State has developed a more traditional treatment: exile. In the West exile is perhaps looked upon as a form of liberty. It ought not to be forgotten that it is also a form of political exclusion; and in the modern world political exclusion is often an initial step towards extermination. The Nazis declared Jews stateless persons before they declared them non-persons. Today displaced persons and refugees are on the point of achieving institutionalized political status. Millions of refugees have been created in East Africa as a by-product of wars of national liberation. Their permanent homes are camps in the Sudan and Somalia, their permanent political benefactors, the United Nations High Commission[1]. They are not alone. Israelis and Palestinians have succeeded in creating a well-nigh insoluble political conflict through a long process of mutual reduction which hinges on the nexus between people and State[2]. Self-determination justifies terrorism, occupation and the denial of the other's claim to human-ness, whose political dimension is citizenry. It is not the only ideology. In countries as disparate as Iran and Cambodia mobilizing elites have set about to remake an entire society, which means of course remaking millions of individuals as well[3]. The consequences are notorious: massive forced internal migrations, torture and repression. And the torture is growing, year by year, country by country, outstripping the past and outstripping fantasy: Brazil, Chile, Argentina, Guatemala, El Salvador, Uruguay, to name but a few countries where torture, assassination, forced military induction, collective guilt and intimidation, even genocide on a local level, have become institutionalized state practices[4]. Every now and then one talks about the democratization of these regimes, just as one talks about the liberalization of the Soviet system, or the transformation of apartheid in South Africa; yet even if such talk were not ideological trappings there is still Keynes' most pertinent remark: in the long run we will all be dead.

It is already, in such dark times, a measure of achievement to list the horror shows and protest against them; but what signifies this growing statism, how to analyse it? At one level one is inclined to qualify it as a reactionary phenomenon, the last hurrah of that part of the world still trapped in the Hobbesian nightmare of underdevelopment, where authoritarian regimes, precisely because of their massive recourse to violence, are the hallmarks of political instability. In this view of modern history, the rise of the democratic state and constitutional government forms part of the institutional complex of citizenship, which has its roots in the long sixteenth century that served as the crucible of capitalist progress. This process was a long and bloody one. Enclosure movements uprooted the peasantry, creating vagabonds and workhouses. Capitalist industrialization impoverished the working-class for a century. The abolition of the Ancien Régime proved violent and sanguinary, not only for the traditional elites but also for the newly enfranchised masses. Where modernization came late, moreover, so too, it is suggested, came fascism. By the time this development had spent its force, five hundred years later, some measure of restraint on the arbitrary power of the sovereign had been achieved. The rule of law and the welfare State have become to some extent the daily option of citizens in Canada, the United States, Western Europe and Japan: life expectancy has increased, people do not live on rooftops, parcels can be sent through the mail with reasonable confidence that customs' officials will not steal their contents. Such was not always the case. For most of human history it probably was not, and for most of the world under the sway of overtly repressive regimes, it probably is not still. Within this perspective, and only within this perspective, can the growing statism of the modernizing yet underdeveloped part of the world be construed as a phenomenon in a long state of transition, harking back to traditional forms of social control that sooner or later will reveal themselves to be incompatible with the course of modernity and progress upon which human history has embarked. Indeed, in the functionalist reading of modern history, the particular institutional complex of statist democracy is the prerequisite to that social and technological innovation wherein freedom and progress, however ambiguous, are also synonymous, and thereby the wave of the future[5].

This reading of history is not implausible, yet the signs are contradictory and disquieting. Keynes' caveat aside, the repressive mechanisms of contemporary States bear little resemblance to the State apparatus of traditional anciens régimes. Sophisticated and methodological, they are rooted in the developments of modern technology and ideology. Not only are the means of torture highly refined, so too are the psychological procedures upon which the practice of such torture depends. Schools of torture now exist to train the practitioners[6]. One can well imagine the degree of psychological sophistication required to prepare them in a world which officially condemns such practices. If the Nazis relied chiefly on ideology and totalitarian isolation to indoctrinate the SS, their contemporary homologues must find such methods clumsy and obsolete, no doubt because inefficient. In this sense, torture has become part of modernity. Nor does the ideology lag far behind. What Orwell described as doublethink and newspeak has become part of official language throughout the world; nor is it merely an impression that we have heard it all before. After the failure of the German workers' revolt in 1953, Brecht wittily pointed out that the lesson for the government was clear: it was time to dissolve the people and elect another one[7]. In 1980 the president of Uruguay commented upon the people's failure to ratify in a referendum the institutionalization of a military dictatorship in much the same terms, labelling it a defeat for the people[8]. It is a measure of the political distance travelled that the later quip came no longer from a poet, but from a president, losing in the process even the solace of irony.

Such ideological manipulation deforms torture politically into therapeutic repression. The more stable yet openly coercive regimes, like the Soviet Union or the Republic of South Africa, can thereby use law and psychiatry to hide the fact that the entire society is based upon an edifice of terror[9]. The edifice is, so to speak, built-in, and the political relevance of this cupboard full of skeletons resides in these regimes' capacities to legitimize such practices in the name of social institutions traditionally associated with welfare and protection. What we are witnessing perhaps is the complete subversion, in the direction of its negative pole, of the historically twinned processes of public welfare and social control which accompanied and justified the rise of the modern State[10]. If so, this development raises serious questions about the whole nature of progress and of the Enlightenment whose offspring it has christened, as well as the drift of the modern State where the elements of social control have hitherto been somewhat restrained. Perhaps, in bitter and ironic commentary upon Marx's vision of communist society, the USSR does indeed represent the resolved enigma of history, presenting to capitalist democracies the future of their own contradictions.

It is a future moreover which cuts across the traditional boundaries of Right and Left. Much as "really existing" socialist societies have usurped the progressive stand in the bourgeois project and incorporated it into their legitimation process, so too have the emerging, total societies of the third world converted socialist ideology. The model of present-day Iran is a case in point. Its spokesmen and its apologists present a nascent and indigenous form of state control, where religious tradition is yoked to modern methods of repression, as both a legitimate model of modernization and critique of western society, godless, materialist and, one might almost add, bourgeois. The arrangement might again almost sound familiar, but there are a few new notes in the refrain: the critique is implicitly progressive, capitalizing on the loss of transcendence in western society and seeking to offer in its place a viable model of modernity. "The great powers fear Islam because it constructs the total man' (Iman Khomeiny). The revolutionary project is not to modernize Islam but to Islamize modernity: a challenge at once to the materialism and to the rationalism which constitutes the West"[11]. The refrain is nonetheless replete with catchwords that in another context were labelled national-socialism: the attack on decadence, the anti-imperialist tinge, the expansionist ring, the call for total mobilization. If fascism can reappear, and this time more overtly in the ideology of modernization, then how to interpret the Nazi experience?[12] History no longer presents itself as irreversible, and Hitlerite Germany not only as one of capitalism's accidents, a by-product of both developmental lag and national specificity. Rather fascism seems also to be a wrong turning point too often taken, a lapse into barbarism that threatens to be the wave of the future and which, by engulfment or by ricochet, threatens to exacerbate those tendencies in the earlier and dominant project of modernization that lend its forms of progress their ambiguous character.

Already in the Great French Revolution, that focal point of the bourgeois project, such tendencies were present, albeit in embryonic form, such that the problem of the French Revolution is even today the problem of the modern State. The revolution of liberty, equality and fraternity paradoxically produced a centralized State, the foundation of a modern administrative elite, a universalist ideology, modern imperialism and the Terror. Liberalism, though haunted from the outside by the social question, was riddled from the outset by its own, internal contradictions. If the revolutionaries sought the overthrow of the Ancien Régime, they also sought to maintain the essential political contours of the relationship between government and the governed. Citizens replaced subjects, but the State retained political power, and the project of freedom and democracy foundered upon the refusal of the revolutionary elites to institute new political relationships outside State forms. Vengeful ruse of the old order, it haunted the revolutionary regime every step of the way, constantly producing its unintended consequences and ultimately sabotaging successive attempts to arrest the course of demolition and found a new order. A case in point: in the initial debates over whether to launch a revolutionary war Robespierre opposed it, justifying his reluctance in a remark that was intuitively prescient, even if he was to ignore its most democratic implications. "For him, the centre of evil was Paris, before Coblenz"[13]. Yet the evil that lay in Paris was not only in the counter-revolutionaries, nor even in the poverty of the masses. It was also the possibility of communal and federative democracy that made its first appearance on the national level. Two years earlier, however, the revolutionary regime had already staked out its position in one of its first ideological constructs that was to be a substitute for spontaneous politics from below: the Fête de la Fédération of July 14, 1790. Conceived in order to hedge in the municipal and federalist revolutions that were emerging parallel to the movement at Paris and Versailles, the Fête de la Fédération revealed symbolically the ultimate transformation of the revolutionary moment of 1789 into its ideological and political outcome: the union of liberty and the people via the nation-state[14]. That union congealed, it became increasingly difficult to resolve any of the successive tensions of the revolution except by a further leap forward, into modernity and into terror.

As the revolutionary dynamic unfolded the political spectrum narrowed and the wars of factions intensified, with the people and their welfare continuously invoked as justification. Hence no faction could afford to be pacific, for pacifism became equated with counter-revolution and treason. The people, conveniently and functionally excluded from the political process, took their revenge upon the elites by indirectly forcing them into political adventures that ended up devouring everyone. What started as a war of defence against European reaction became an annexationist military adventure to impose a universal republic on the peoples of Europe[15]. Liberty, unrealisable at home, became exported abroad. Its denouement emerged under the Directory in the form of Napoleon's pillage of Italy[16]: ideology and imperialism uniting to foreshadow the spectre of twentieth-century totalitarianism as fascist gangs looted foreign art treasures and *Stalin's* armies imposed liberation upon the hapless peoples of Eastern Europe. As in the later period so too at the inception of modern politics the inability to resolve the tensions of democracy was not solved by exporting them abroad[17]. The chickens came home to roost in the popular insurrections of the Parisian *sans-culottes* and the Vendéen peasantry, insurrections that elicited reactions on the part of the revolutionary elites similar to, in retrospect, contemporary barbarism. When the Commune of Paris, for example, approached the Convention on May 25, 1793 to demand the liberation of some of their leaders, the Girondin Ismard threatened any future insurrection with the destruction of Paris on such a scale that one would have to search afterwards beneath the banks of the Seine to see if it had ever existed, and this in the name of the national interest[18]. Two months later a Jacobin convention voted the systematic destruction of the Vendée: forests, crops, cattle seized and destroyed, women, children and the elderly deported into the interior[19]. Over a century later similar practices were to emerge in Hitler's scorched-earth policy and Stalin's liquidation of the Russian peasantry; only now the methods measured up to the ideological ranting of the elites, racism and the dust-bin theory of history replacing the earlier incantations of liberty, progress and the republic.

Yet the underlying dynamic bears too great a similarity to ignore the fascist and communist strands that exist in the original liberal project whose common origin lies in the insistence on the State's monopoly to define the limits of popular political participation. In a certain sense the problem of mass democracy was the fundamental problem of the French Revolution[20]. Its Statist resolution could only result in the transformation of king into nation, individual into masses and politics into ideology and administration. The French Revolution produced the Great Terror when it was least needed, and the ironic spectacle of an anticlerical parliament voting the French people's recognition of the Supreme Being and the soul's immortality[21]. In terms of institutional reform, the Thermidorean Convention and the Directory put into place a series of institutions of higher learning that laid the basis for the technocratic class that has since been indispensable to the administration of the modern State. In that respect too the French Revolution was only a beginning, the integration of the Institute into the constitution of the Directory with a special section devoted to the moral and political sciences being a first, if incomplete testimony to the growing importance of a trained mandarinate and their scientific rationality to modern government[22]. Viewed in this light, however, the bourgeois nature of the French Revolution goes beyond its somewhat partial role in the preparation of nineteenth-century French capitalism to underscore a longer project of social control, of which capitalism constitutes an historical moment and the State a pivotal institution[23]. That project is also the project of modernity, hence its initial rational, emancipatory and progressive appearance. Yet it also has an ideological kernel that festers around the management of democracy. Hence its persistent evocation by elites of all ideological stripes, and hence too its persistent ambiguity: progress but also regress, increased autonomy but also increased control.

It is this very ambiguity that opens up the interpretive difficulties in the analysis of the modern State. The *dirigisme* incipient in the early bourgeois State has mushroomed to the point where little remains of the State that is specifically bourgeois. Following this line of thought, fascism becomes a moment in the development of the modern State rather than a point of regression in the development of capitalism, a social order which favours the emergence of a technobureaucracy functionally necessary to the administration of that State[24]. Such a perspective would also explain why at different historical moments and in different political colours, modernity has displayed a remarkable similarity. Where government is proclaimed for the people, but in actual fact kept in the hands of its elites, it is hardly surprising that increasing emphasis is laid on the cultural revolution as the heart of modernization. A sure indication of the continued presence of domination, this ideological formulation has been characteristic of regimes as ostensibly disparate as Nazi Germany, Maoist China and Islamic Iran. What one author has described for Latin America:

"No doubt there also exists, within the reformist or revolutionary movements, of a christian or humanist inspiration, even beneath the uniforms and the cilices, a not inconsiderable current which emphasizes the necessity of arriving at a veritable emancipation, full democracy, effective participation and real responsibility for the producers, workers and peasants. But it is only a counter-current, too often lost in a vast confusion, of the general tendency which aims at and relies on state power as the sole source of change and authority. The social origin and character formation of these activists make it difficult to see at the outset how irreconcilable and irreducible these two aproaches are.
If we do not restrict ourselves to the phrases and declarations of intention, but trace the behaviour and dealings of each member of the new avant-gardes, we are forced to acknowledge that the general rule which inspires them is to arrive at a total mobilisation of resources and manpower, to see to their maximum utilisation, to assure their discipline and their management, to extort from them the greatest

possible yield and to arm an economy of combat. Agrarian reform to favour the creation of a worker proletariat, the rational employment of the productive capacity to make possible investments which reinforce industrial potential, multiple organisations to assure labour productivity and discipline: such are the essential orientations. With an appeal to enthusiasm and to volunteers at the beginning, but very quickly thereafter a recourse to diverse methods of constraint.

A programme which could be qualified as socialist, for it permits in words the analgamation of millenarian aspirations with the requirements of planning. A method which could just as well be designated in other terms, less heady and even, quite frankly, dangerous, if we were willing to push our curiosity to the point of asking who commands, who benefits and who gets to use surplus-value"[25].

another has recently confirmed for Ethiopia:

"In 1981, the members of the COPTE (the Commission on Organisation of the Ethiopian Workers' Party), which already has the appearance of a party, could be classified as follows: peasants, 1.2%; workers, 2.9%; teachers, civil servants, members of the army and other sectors of society, 95%. After a special effort at recruitment and a change in the criteria of admission, the composition had become by October 1982: peasants, 3.3%, workers, 21.7%; intelligentsia, civil servants, member of the army and other sections of society, 75%. The figures speak for themselves. The COPTE is to be transformed into a veritable party on the occasion of the revolution's tenth anniversary, and it is not difficult to see in these conditions which social class holds and will hold power in Addis-Ababa. It is no chance accident that the celebrated writer Bealu Girma was divested of his functions as general secretary of the Ministry of Information and his latest book confiscated and banned: in it he accused the new bureaucrats of seeking only women and cars and compared them to Milovan Djilas' 'new class' "[26].

In the West the new class is thriving and the control mechanisms increasing. It is perhaps more evident at first in the contemporary capitalist State's foreign relations: the use of international monetary institutions to maintain both third-world dependency and third-world Bonapartism[27]; the export abroad of schools of torture and techniques of pacification that have extended and refined what Hoche implemented for the Directory in the Vendée[28]; the increasing resort to ideological obfuscation and hyperbole, where incursion means invasion, national security, imperialism, and free elections a licence for repression[29]. Such developments, however, are not without their boomerang effect on the politics of the capitalist heartlands. Life there is becoming, for all the development, in many respects more difficult and anxiety-ridden. The crisis is taking root, shattering dreams and lives. More people are on welfare or unemployed. Young people have few prospects for jobs. Birth rates are down. Families are splitting up. Borders are closing. The State is tightening up welfare provisions[30], but even as it seeks to ease its way out of welfare programmes it moves to interfere in new areas of social activity, or in old areas with new regulations: sexuality, health care, demography, immigration, space. In the Federal Republic of Germany the government has instituted policies whereby women who do not abort a child will receive a considerable payment from the State. In Canada what was once a comparatively liberal immigration policy has changed to the point where it is very difficult for foreigners to immigrate into Canada unless they are either very wealthy or particularly qualified[31]. In the United States the government is pouring billions of dollars into military research with the aim of transporting nuclear war into space. Underlying these and other initiatives is an international economic rivalry between the United States, Western Europe and Japan where a race for technological supremacy is promoting militarism at an increasing rate[32]. Racism and violence have returned to haunt the constitutional democracies in forms as divergent as right-wing political movements (the FN in France), video musicals (Thriller), inexplicable out-breaks of homicide, and television. Anthony Hecht has caught the mood well in his poem, "It Out-Herods Herod, Pray You, Avoid It":

Tonight my children hunch
Toward their Western, and are glad
As, with a Sunday punch,
The Good casts out the bad.

And in their fairy tales
The warty giant and witch
Get sealed in doorless jails
And the match-girl strikes it rich.

I've made myself a drink.
The giant and witch are set
To bust out of the clink
When my children have gone to bed.

All frequencies are loud
With signals of despair;
In flash and morse they crowd
The rondure of the air.

For the wicked have grown strong,
Their numbers mock at death,
Their cow brings forth its young,
Their bull engendereth.

Their very fund of strength,
Satan, bestrides the globe;
He stalks its breadth and length
And finds out even Job.

Yet by quite other laws
My children make their case;
Half God, half Santa Claus,
But with my voice and face,

A hero comes to save
The poorman, beggarman, thief,
And make the world behave
And put an end to grief.

And that their sleep be sound
I say this childermas
Who could not, at one time,
Have saved them from the gas[33].

Beneath the anxiety however lies perhaps the suspicion that it is all some-how unjustified, the crisis, the austerity, the untold repression on a world-wide scale, the sense that perhaps the real nature of the crisis is that of contemporary social organization in the face of current knowledge and resources, wealth and energy. The more dominant and immediately perceived reaction is one of frustration and powerlessness, reinforced by the admission of élites in the State and the private sector that they too are powerless to act in the face of international pressures that they cannot control. The panic produced paradoxically feeds the desire for control, nourishing in turn those social forces that will make a more authoritarian development on the part of the Western States a not wholly unthinkable or unlikely prospect[34]. The automation of entire factories, the introduction of robots, the increased reliance on computers has made work as we know it obsolescent, but society still runs on the cash nexus, making work as we know it still necessary even if redundant[35]. The division of labour within the societies at the capitalist centre will thus come to resemble the division of labour, and rewards, within the current international order: a vast underclass in relative poverty ruled and managed by an international elite whose very existence, not to mention privilege, will rest on the maintenance of a system of control in which the State, or some modified form of it, will continue to play an important role[36]. Hints of this possible scenario can already be seen in a rising proportion, if reports are to be believed, of certified educated people who are functionally illiterate.

The pernicious element in this scenario is that, though the technobureaucracy remains, power becomes diffused throughout society, masking the elements of control that persist and fueling the impression that the State is dead. It is an element that systems theorists have themselves described, though they have regarded the progressive action evolution of society as constitutive of its very freedom: "This implies, on the one hand, a freedom of action for its individual component member units, but on the other hand, new mechanisms of control which make the functioning of such freedoms feasible at increasingly generalized levels"[37]. This is a not inaccurate description of how power operates and is subjectively perceived in contemporary society, especially in those representations diffused by the media. Political discussions invariably tend to take on a therapeutic hue. The animators are invariably progressive. The participants are appropriately dogmatic or cool. But as the character in the Man Who Fell To Earth said, (or something like this): "Television tells you many things, but it doesn't tell you the whole truth". Nothing does perhaps, but there is a method to this particular madness, the method of the order maniacs, the working of the definition of the situation into the current paradigm of control. People see a world being constructed before their very eyes, the social construction of reality which nonetheless escapes their control even as they try to manage it, or only participate. Given the structured inequality of power and resources, control is a dream whose achievement is necessarily reserved for the few; but as long as the vast majority consent to the definition, seek salvation on its terms, the system of control will continue even as it seems a system out of control[38]: society as its own cybernetic action system.

This admittedly is one of the more lugubrious scenarios, and truly Orwellian. It will require certain innovations and certain convergences on an international level — east and west, north and south, State and multinational corporation — in a revamping and restructuring of the already centuries-old process known as modernization, but it is not total fantasy except in an etymological sense. There is, however, another possible storyline, more in conformity with the functionalist and marxist traditions that have tended to see, each in its own way but in common historical accord, a slow but definite unfolding of history as progress and freedom at increasing levels of feasibility. In this evolutionist version, the more complex societies, because more adaptable, necessarily represent the future, in which autonomy and control are, and will remain, indissolubly linked; but the progress, however ambiguous, is nonetheless real, as is individual autonomy, however much accompanied by new and sophisticated forms of control. One need only look at mortality figures over the past five hundred years, or the increased openness around questions of sex and gender. Even control and its concomitant scientific rationality have certain points in their favour, being the material basis for the relative contemporary degrees of freedom, for the possibilities of unforeseeable lines of development (space travel with all its implications) and for a state of existence in which anxiety is eventually, realistically reduced. The political inheritors of this perspective are social-democracy and all its variants: hence their defence of the State, constitutional and controlled, as one indispensable element in a mediated society opening into freedom; and hence their realism.

This perspective is not implausible, but a nagging doubt persists that in this time frame, we certainly will all be dead. The doubt also remains because of the very ambiguity of freedom and progress in the world's more liberal zones and the questions they continue to elicit. Choice is widened, yet it seems to make no difference, for the impression lingers that the choice, from sex to politics, is in reality no choice; and all the gadgetry in the world, while it has made household tasks individually easier, seems part of a process whereby child-raising as a whole has become more difficult[39]. Perhaps in part this is due to the greater time people in industrialized countries now have to devote themselves to interpersonal relationships, that most inscrutable of social domains. Yet perhaps it is also a consequence of a process in which each advance in human endeavor becomes the next link in a chain of social control rather than one more step taken to reorganize social life, simplify the domain of necessity and free time from its dominion. No sooner is human activity released from one area of drudgery than it is channelled or seduced into others whose mastery or enjoyment can only be achieved at the price of continued sacrifice, subordination or conflict. This holds as much for what goes on within the individual psyche as between the individual and the collectivity: the society of repressive desublimation[40], of spectacular time, in which

"... individual life as yet has no history. The pseudo-events which rush by in spectacular dramatizations have not been lived by those informed of them; moreover they are lost in the inflation of their hurried replacement at every throb of the spectacular machinery. Furthermore, what is really lived has no relation to the official irreversible time of society and is in direct opposition to the pseudo-cyclical rhythm of the consumable by-product of this time. This individual experience of seperate daily life remains without language, without concept, without critical access to its own past which has been recorded nowhere. It is not communicated. It is not understood and is forgotten to the profit of the false spectacular memory of the unmemorable."[41]

The disagreement between, what for lack of better terms, can be called the positivist and critical theory perspectives hinges thus in part on a disagreement about the facts, in part on a disagreement about how to interpret them. The dominant political trends each perspective discerns nonetheless underlines what is being increasingly banished in the contemporary world: utopia and the principle of hope which the utopian spirit energetically brandishes. At the heart of the political debate over the nature of the State is the question whether a mediated society without a State but committed to freedom and, yes, even progress is possible. It is at the heart of the debate between social democracy and anarchism, between realpolitik and utopia. Yet for all their realism and empiricism, positivism and social democracy seem to forget that the contemporary State has emerged historically from the subordination and integration of democracy's utopian elements[42], while the solutions they propose seem only to reproduce the problems they purport to resolve[43]. Perhaps it is the best we have to offer, but perhaps it is not merely wishful thinking to point out that only a fundamental transformation of the structure of social organization holds out the promise of improvement on a scale equal to the task. Today perhaps more than ever, "regarding the concrete utopian possibility, dialectics is the ontology of the wrong state of things"[44].

Fortunately there are people and groups who continue to protest, who refuse to accept things as they are and who insist, in order for there to be some kind of future, on keeping the past from being obliterated by the present. They are the people among others who form Amnesty International, who join the peace movement, who maintain the struggle for women's rights, who work hard in the Third World, who still ask questions about the wrong state of things and seek in their answers a measure of truth that does not flinch before the vastness of the task. They would perhaps agree that "the critique of ideology... is central"[45] and try to live it in the face of their own contradictions. To do more is the task of politics, and to clarify the task is the task of theory.

NOTES

[1] United Nations High Commission for Refugees, *Refugees*, January 1984, Geneva.
[2] See N. Caplan, *Futile Diplomacy*, (2 vols), London, Cass, 1983, 1984.

3 For Guatemala see America's Watch, "Extermination in Guatemala", New York Review of Books, June 2, 1983, p. 13-16. For Uruguay see Le Monde Diplomatique, December, 1983, p. 9-13. For Argentina see Le Monde Diplomatique, October, 1983, p. 22-27. See also Amnesty International, *Rapport 1981*, EFAI, Paris, 1982 and Amnesty International, *Les 'disparus'*, Seuil, Paris, 1981.
4 For Iran see the articles on La Révolution Islamique Iranienne, Le Monde Diplomatique, April, 1984, p. 12-18; for Cambodia see N. Chomsky and E. Herman, *The Political Economy of Human Rights* (2 vols), Montreal, Black Rose Books, 1979, esp. vol 2, although the point of the work is more to assess the role of the Western press than to offer an exhaustive account of events in Cambodia.
5 Though written from quite different theoretical and political perspectives, there is considerable agreement about where and when the transformation to modernity occurred. See for example, I. Wallerstein, *The Modern World System*, Academic Press, N.Y. and London, 1974 and T. Parsons, *Social Systems and the Evolution of Action Theory*, Free Press, Glencoe, Illinois, 1977. For the equation of modernity and progress, however ambiguous or reluctant, see for example, F. Braudel, *Capitalism and Material Life, 1400-1800*, (tr. M. Kochan) London, 1973 and P. Chaunu, *La civilisation de l'Europe des lumières*, Champs Flammarion, Paris, 1982. For caveats about the nature of progress and modernization see E.P. Thompson, *The Making of the English Working Class*, Penguin, 1968 and B. Moore Jr., *The Social Origins of Dictatorship and Democracy*, Boston, 1966.
6 Chomsky and Herman, *op. cit.*, ch. 2.
7 Quoted in H. Arendt, "Bertolt Brecht" in Arendt, *Men In Dark Times*, Johnathan Cape, London, 1970, p. 213.
8 E.G. Bermejo, "La décennie honteuse", Le Monde Diplomatique, December, 1983, p. 11.
9 See Amnesty International, *Rapport 1981*, op. cit., p. 33-9 for the Republic of South Africa, p. 383-92 for the USSR.
10 See for example, J. Donzelot, *La police des familles*, Paris, Minuit, 1977, for one account of this process.
11 J.-L. Herbert, "La force mobilisatrice d'une spiritualité" in Le Monde Diplomatique, April, 1984, p. 17.
12 For a review of this question see P. Ayçoberry, *La question nazie*, Seuil, Paris, 1979.

[13] F. Furet and D. Richet, *La Révolution française*, Marabout, Verviens, Belgium, 1979, p. 149.
[14] Ibid., p. 112-3.
[15] Ibid., p. 184-5.
[16] Ibid., p. 382-3.
[17] See Arendt's comments on the way the nineteenth-century European imperialist adventure rebounded with a vengeance against the exporting countries in H. Arendt, *The Origins of Totalitarianism*, N.Y., 1951.
[18] Furet and Richet, *op. cit.*, p. 198.
[19] Ibid., p. 225.
[20] See H. Sklar, *Trilateralism*, Black Rose Books, Montreal, 1980, esp. A. Wolfe, "Capitalism Shows Its Face: Giving Up On Democracy", p. 295-307 for a discussion of the Trilateral Task Force's report on The Crisis of Democracy which signals an "excess of democracy" as a major contemporary problem.
[21] Furet and Richet, *op. cit.*, p. 248.
[22] Ibid., p. 467-70.
[23] For a truly radical exposition of this argument see G. Debord, *The Society of the Spectacle*, Black and Red, Detroit, 1977, translated from the French, *La société du spectacle*, Paris, Buchet-Chastel, 1967, Champ Libre, 1971; at the same time my reading of the French Revolution owes much to F. Furet, *Penser la Révolution française*, Gallimard, Paris, 1978, whose analysis of the French Revolution offers a superb discussion of the relationship between revolution and ideology and raises at nearly every page important questions about the nature of modern politics.
[24] L. Lanza, "Fascism and Techno-bureaucracy" in *Our Generation*, Montreal, vol 12, no. 1, summer 1977, p. 45-57. For a lengthier discussion on the technobureaucracy see Un collectif de recherche anarchiste, *Les nouveaux patrons: onze études sur la techno-bureaucratie*, Geneva, Editions Noir, 1979, translated from the Italian, *I Nuovi Padroni*, Edizione Antistato, Milan, 1978.
[25] L. Mercier-Vega, *La révolution par l'Etat*, Payot, Paris, 1978, p. 10-11.
[26] O. Kapeliouk, "Quand le paysan est tenu à l'écart des décisions politiques" in Le Monde Diplomatique, April, 1984, p. 11.
[27] See for example G. Corn, "Une fructueuse renégociation des dettes" in Le Monde Diplomatique, September, 1983,

p. 3; F. Clairmonte, "Le pouvoir méconnu", Ibid., p. 2; Chomsky and Herman, *op. cit.*

[28] Furet and Richet, *op. cit.*, p. 339 and the ideology of pacification so widely present in the American conduct of the Viet Nam War.

[29] The U.S. invasion of Cambodia was an incursion. The name of the principal political prison in Uruguay is Liberdàd. See also Chomsky and Herman, *op. cit.*, esp. vol 2.

[30] E. Shragge, "A Libertarian Response to the Welfare State" in *Our Generation*, vol. 15, nu. 4, spring 1983, p. 36-47.

[31] In the Federal Republic of Germany the government would like to send a good number of that country's Turkish immigrant workers back to Turkey, while a majority of West Germans favour the departure of these gast arbeiter whom they now hold responsible for unemployment. See L. Vekilli, "Turken raus'?", in Le Monde Diplomatique, December, 1983.

[32] P. Chamsol, "Cette guerre que nul ne veut...", Le Monde Diplomatique, April, 1984, p. 1, 26-7.

[33] A. Hecht, *The Hard Hours*, Atheneum, N.Y., 1978, p. 67-8.

[34] For one such version see R. Heilbroner, *An Inquiry into the Human Prospect*, Norton, N.Y., 1979.

[35] For an initial exploration about the possibilities of the reduction of work see Adret, *Travailler deux heures par jour*, Seuil, Paris, 1977.

[36] See N. Laurin-Frenette, "Les intellectuels et l'Etat" in *Sociologie et sociétés*, vol. XV, no. 1, April, 1983, p. 121-9 for an initial and important exploration of the contemporary relationship between intellectuals and the State within the dominant paradigm of power and control.

[37] Parsons, *op. cit.*, p. 130.

[38] H. Marcuse, *One-Dimensional Man*, Boston, Beacon, 1964.

[39] See N. Laurin-Frenette, "Féminisme et Anarchisme: quelques éléments théoriques et historiques pour une analyse de la relation entre le Mouvement des femmes et l'Etat" in Y. Cohen (ed.) *Femmes et politique*, Le Jour, Montréal, 1981, p. 167. For an abridged English version of this article see *Our Generation*, vol. 15, no. 2, summer 1982.

40 H. Marcuse, *op. cit.*
41 G. Debord, *op. cit.*, section 157.
42 M. Bookchin *The Ecology of Freedom*, Cheshire Press, Palo Alto, California, 1982, esp. chs. 7 and 8.
43 For an example of what "the Left" has to offer see R. Debray, *La Puissance et les Rêves*, Gallimard, Paris, 1984; and for an interesting critique see C. De Brie, "Vers une Realpolitik de Gauche" in Le Monde Diplomatique, April, 1984, p. 28.
44 T. Adorno, *Negative Dialectics*, (tr. E.B. Ashton), N.Y., Seabury Press, 1973, p. 11.
45 Ibid., p. 148.

Job's Comfort: The State and the Arts in 1984

by George Woodcock

> ... the Lord gave, and the
> Lord hath taken away...*Job*.1:2

Relations between artists and institutions are at best uneasy, and can never be otherwise, since the very act of creation in many of the arts, notably writing and painting, is inevitably a solitary one. In the case of the performing artist, its takes on a collective character, the partnership which brings the work to final fruition — whether it is a play or an opera or an orchestral composition or a ballet — is likely to be much nearer to the loose collaboration of like-minded people exemplified in the affinity group that was the favourite organizational form of the anarchists than to the kind of rigid organization which governmental bureaucracies favour and which, to the detriment of revolutionary hopes, is adopted by authoritarian-minded radicals whose aim is usually to replace by a *coup d'état* one type of coercive institution by another.

This is why artists are not much better off in their relations with the modern State, whether they live in countries that are called communist or countries that are called capitalist. In both situations the pseudo-benevolent interference of the State in the arts has come to be regarded as desirable; indeed, it is widely believed, in Canada and in the western European democracies as much as in Russia and its eastern European satellites, that in the modern world the arts could not function or survive without such interference.

In this essay I am proceeding from the viewpoint that art, however individualized and isolated the processes of its creation may be, is a social activity. Since, no matter how idiosyncratic and apparently obscure it may be, art is always in the last resort an attempt at communication, the situation could hardly be otherwise. Artist-and-audience is one of the symbiotic relations that form part of the natural network of any community. One can go beyond this and maintain that a community finds its definition and the expression of its real nature through the works of its artists, and that this happens as much through the creations of those who retreat into solitude to write their poems or paint their pictures as through the achievements of those whose interpretative activities, as singers and actors, as dancers and musicians, demand the participation of a collectivity, first as the performing group and then as the witnessing participants; a community often survives only through the works of its artists which act as Malraux's voices of silence, communicating its vision of existence to later generations.

But if artists of all kinds give expression to the identity of the community as well as satisfying those aesthetic needs which newspapermen are inclined to neutralize by dismissing them as "entertainment," this means that the community owes the artist its support. The artist's work has to be recognized as of equal social value to occupations that are obviously necessary in material terms — like that of the baker or the truck farmer or the electrician.

In fact, in pre-modern cultures where the political strand was weak and where organic community relations came into being without the emergence of an organized State structure, the role of artists was accepted as the remembrancers of myth and history, and so was the need for them to be supported by the society which depended on them to define through images and symbols its relationship with the natural world. One need not go beyond Canada to find an example; it is there in the culture of the Kwakiutl Indians of what is now British Columbia, whose summers, before the white men destroyed their civilization were spent gathering and preserving food and trading, and whose winters were devoted to the lavish community ceremonials of a society which had hierarchy without government. The Kwakiutl dance fraternities and the individual chiefs provided their artists — carvers and painters and constructors of ingenious theatrical machines — with an abundant living in return for their indispensable contributions to the great dramatic choreographies of the winter dances and the potlatches through which the peoples of the coast lived out their myths and defined their collective as well as their individual personae. Each man or woman in such a culture danced their own dance which confirmed their position in the social order, but the mask they wore, the rattle they flourished, the pole they might dedicate, would be the work of a professional whose skills and whose knowledge of the myths were revered, and whom the community sustained without question.

During the middle ages, in the earlier stages of our own western civilization, urban communities were held together partly by their Christian faith and partly by the particular variant of mutual aid which, as Kropotkin and later writers like Lewis Mumford have so admirably shown, was manifested in the guilds of the great free cities that provided a counterbalance to the strength of feudalism in the rural hinterland. The Gothic cathedrals that still tower over the towns of France and Britain and the Rhineland were the great manifestations of communal art in this period, in which religious fraternities and guilds of artisans and artists collaborated to manifest, in architecture and sculpture and painting, in stained glass and textiles of unprecedented richness, the spirit of the age and the beliefs of its people. There was little distinction between artists and artisans, and the painter or sculptor, like any other craftsman, worked and was sustained within a guild structure, completely outside the rudimentary organization of the feudal state. It took the artist through the grades of apprenticeship, journeying and mastery, and gave him not merely a recognized status within the community but also the assurance of an adequate living so long as he maintained the standards of the art. The sustaining of the arts by the fraternities and guilds which were the most characteristic social organizations of the period, declined after the Reformation, though they survived in an attenuated form in Canada right down to the present century, for it was in church construction and decoration that the visual arts first appeared in Québec, and some of the greatest Canadian artists were sustained in this way by the people of French-speaking parishes, including Ozias Leduc — arguably the first truly modern painter in Canada — who made his living by church decoration, and Paul-Emile Borduas, who was his assistant and pupil.

Parallel with the church-cum-guild strain of religious art that dominated the cities and monasteries of the middle ages, ran a strain of aristocratic art manifested largely in the epics of mediaeval chivalry like the *Chanson de Roland* and in the songs of the troubadours which expressed the stylized eroticism of the late mediaeval feudal courts. As the arts became more individualized from the Italian *quattrocento* onwards, with the concept of the artist as personality beginning to emerge, the patronage of artists by individual noblemen and magnates became the custom. Princelings like Lorenzo de Medici and Sigismondo Malatesta, monarchs like Henry VIII (the patron of Holbein) and Charles I (the patron of Van Dyck) are now remembered largely because of the artists they befriended.

This shift from the community support of the middle ages, when the artist was actually one of the guild or fraternity that sustained him and hence tended towards the anonymity of the mediaeval craftsman, to the patronage of the Renaissance and the Baroque period, balanced the emergence of the artist as an individual, whose personal vision was recognized in contrast to the collective vision of the past, with an insecurity bred of dependence on the caprices of a single patron rather than on the support of a reliable if somewhat conservative community. There is a harrowing letter from the great sixteenth century humanist Erasmus to one of his friends which shows uncertainties now endured by men whose independence drove them out of the security of monastic establishments into reliance on the support of unreliable individuals in a situation where the infrastructure of the modern world of literature and the arts did not exist even in rudimentary form.

"So I entreat and implore you, dear Batt, if you have a single spark of your former affection for me, to give your most earnest consideration to saving me. With your agreeable, easy-going disposition, you can possibly believe that you have left me well off; however, I seem to be in a worse state of ruin than ever before, since X offers no bounty, my lady merely extends promises from day to day, and the bishop goes so far as to turn his back upon me, while the abbot bid me be of good hope. In the meantime, not a soul comes forward to give, save only X, whom I have already squeezed so dry, poor fellow, that he has not a penny more to give me... At the same time, I have many thoughts to ponder: Where shall I flee, without a rag to my back? What if I fall ill? Granted that nothing of this kind happens, what will I be able to achieve in the literary field without access to books? What can I hope to do if I leave Paris? And finally, what will be the use of literary productions if I have no recognized position to back them? Will monsters like the person I encountered at Saint-Omer be able to laugh at me, calling me a prater?"

Erasmus stands at an important historical turning point, and we can read his letter two ways. He lived in an era when the corporate patronage of church and guild was coming to an end and a modern milieu of literature and the arts with its infrastructure of publishing houses and art galleries and periodicals and — eventually — arts councils financed by governments, was still far in the future. Yet his letter is by no means archaic in the anxieties it projects. One can imagine a Canadian counterpart being written in 1984 by some woebegone author turned down for a grant, with individuals replaced by institutions, with an impoverished independent publishing house taking the place of squeezed-dry X, and the CBC, the Canada Council, and one or two provincial arts councils taking the roles of "my lady", the bishop and the abbot. Perhaps contemporary Canadian artists no longer endure the acuter humiliations that Erasmus suffered in grovelling to private patrons, but there are still some who have now become so dependent on public grants that they are vulnerable to any shift in the economic or political wind that makes a government decide to trim its cultural programmes.

The difference between Erasmus's day and our own is of course that the State is now deeply involved in the arts, in "democratic" just as much as in totalitarian countries. The shift began almost two centuries ago in revolutionary France. The Bourbon kings, and especially Louis XIV, had patronised artists in the old feudal way, for their own personal glorification; otherwise their interference in the arts had been negative, censoring content rather than form, and not doing that very successfully, for Beaumarchais managed to get his radically-oriented play, *Le Mariage de Figaro,* produced in 1784, five years before the

Revolution, largely because he had the personal backing of the Queen, Marie Antoinette. But during the period of Jacobin ascendancy between 1792 and 1794 the Robespierrian Committee of Public Safety turned its ominous attention to the artists, and not only encouraged them to produce works that would glorify the Revolution, of which the most celebrated surviving examples are the vast sycophantic canvases of Jacques-Louis David, but also deliberately promoted a neoclassical style which became official and from which artists would deviate at their peril. David survived the downfall of Robespierre to put his grandiose talents at the disposal of the dictator Napoleon, and art was now used for the glorification of the Empire, but the idea of fostering an official style dissolved in the general atmosphere of imperial eclecticism that was manifested in the gathering into the Louvre of artistic masterpieces from all ages and places, in all manners and styles. Art at this stage was used mainly as an ornament rather than as an instrument of the State.

In general, during the nineteenth century, the prevalent economic doctrines of *laisser faire* "liberalism" led to the State avoiding involvement in the arts, whose value bourgeois philistinism in any case tended to depreciate. Lord Melbourne expressed the prevalent attitude of political leaders when he remarked, on the occasion of the painter Benjamin Robert Haydon's suggestion that he set up a fund to assist painters, "God help the Minister who meddles in art." Art, like industry, was allowed to drift with the market, with the result that some writers and painters, like Trollope and Arnold Bennett, like Lord Leighton and Picasso, became rich on their earnings, as did their publishers and dealers, and others, like Vincent Van Gogh and the poet Francis Thompson, lived in poverty and died in despair.

Patronage in this era was replaced by accumulation; the *noblesse oblige* that might lead eighteenth century princelings to take the risk of supporting living artists was replaced by the many-sided avarice of the industrial tycoon who collected as commodities the works of recognized artists, living occasionally but usually dead, using them to enhance his credit when alive and to preserve his memory through suitable legacies when he was dead. Receiving such legacies of art from the past was one of the few positive ways in which during this period the State remained active in the arts. Negatively it manifested its awareness of them through censorship of various kinds, in the democracies managed indirectly through laws regarding obscenity and libel, and in autocratic countries like Tsarist Russia by an open supervision of all writings. Considering that, unlike the Russians, they developed no specialized bureaucracy for carrying out censorship, the democracies showed themselves remarkably active in making life difficult for writers whose works — — prosecuted then — are now regarded as literary classics, like Flaubert's *Madame Bovary,* Baudelaire's *Les Fleurs du Mal,* D.H. Lawrence's *The Rainbow* and *Lady Chatterley's Lover,* and James Joyce's *Ulysses.* All these works were condemned for in one way or another being too explicit in their discussion of sex, and shifts in social mores would eventually make them acceptable, at least outside fundamentalist circles, just as the erosion of religious beliefs had earlier made innocuous works that had formerly been banned as heretical, as Voltaire's writings were in Québec under French rule.

It was the Russian censorship, under the Romanov autocrats, a thoroughgoing one embracing moral, religious and political criteria, that had the most lasting consequences and offered lessons from which the totalitarian regimes that emerged after the collapse of the Tsarist regime did not fail to profit. The great Russian writers of the nineteenth and early twentieth century were mainly dissident in their political attitudes. Even conservative writers like Dostoevsky and Gogol in their own ways found much to criticize in the corruption of the regime, and recognizing that if they criticized explicitly they would not even get into print, all writers learnt to do so obliquely, by allusions and inferences their readers would understand. Turgenev's *Sportsman's Sketches* was a prime early example, an apparently innocuous book of tales about shooting trips in which the narrator described the people he encountered in the countryside and demonstrated that Russian peasants were in temper and intelligence very much like other men and so undermined the main justifications for the retention of the institution of serfdom.

There is no doubt that by translating their convictions of the wrongness of the Tsarist system into the imaginative forms of fiction, poetry and drama, the Russian writers offered a powerful body of implied criticism of the regime, a criticism that helped weaken public acceptance among educated people and thus to prepare the situation in which change became possible. However much they might have rejected the consequences, which Dostoevsky for one saw with a great deal of accuracy, leading Russian writers like Tolstoy and Turgenev, quite apart from declared revolutionaries like Maxim Gorki, must be regarded among the precursors of the revolution of 1917, even if not of the Bolshevik coup.

There is no doubt that the authoritarians who seized power in that coup learnt from the role played by the arts during the Tsarist period. They recognized that artistic subversion is as much a matter of form as of content, and that it can often gain rather than lose effectiveness by obliquity. Early on they decided to control the arts with a double aim: to prevent subversion of the kind that had occurred under the preceding regime and to use the arts for their own propaganda purposes. In this respect as in others the new totalitarians showed themselves more efficient than their autocratic predecessors. There was a surge of formal experimentation in the years immediately after 1917, by artists for whom revolution meant liberation on all levels, but by the mid-twenties the persecution of avant-garde trends was under way and party discipline was increasingly imposed on writers' and artists' organizations, while officially inspired trends like Proletcult and Socialist Realism put an end to experiment and imposed formal standards — the beginnings of totalitarian art. Any kind of free association between artists was virtually brought to an end by the adoption by the Communist Party's Central Committee of a resolution "Concerning the Reconstruction of Literary and Artistic Organizations". Writers like Yesenin and Mayakovsky had by this time been driven to suicide by the destruction of their hopes for a freely revolutionary art. From now on writers who did not conform were merely liquidated, as happened to the novelist Isaac Babel and the poet Osip Mandelstam, who were among the first real victims of the spirit of 1984.

The other totalitarian realms of the interwar years, in Italy and Germany, followed the same course as Russia in their treatment of the arts. Formal experimentation became anathema, and modernist art of all kinds was persecuted in Germany as "degenerate" just as it was persecuted in Russia as "individualist". Public art in buildings and monuments grandiosely celebrated the imperial ambitions of the regimes, and writers were ominously encouraged to project the prevalent ideologies; like Socialist Realism in Russia, the styles favoured in both Germany and Italy reverted to the worst kind of nineteenth century academic art, whose formal conservatism made it more malleable by those whose aims were primarily propagandist than any kind of experimental art could be.

The real point of Orwell's *Nineteen Eighty Four* is not that totalitarian regimes are what they are; by 1949 when his novel was published what had happened under Nazism and Fascism and what was still happening in Russia under Communism were well known. Orwell's actual intent was to tell us that totalitarian tendencies had already entered into the systems that proclaimed themselves the defenders of freedom. The lust for power was like a virus that — Orwell agreed with the anarchists — could strike anywhere, and it could lead dissimilar societies to similar ends. This he had already hinted years before in the dramatic last scene of *Animal Farm* in which the bewildered animals look through the windows of the farmhouse where the ruling pigs are entertaining the visiting human beings:

"Twelve voices were shouting in anger, and they were all alike. No question, now, what had happened to the faces of the pigs. The creatures outside looked from pig to man, and from man to pig, and from pig to man again; but already it was impossible to say which was which."

The very circumstances of modern war, in which individual fates and the general economic and social structure must be subordinated to the military machine, are of their nature totalitarian, and in every country that was involved in World War II there was a marked and irreversible trend towards the interference of the State in the lives of the people. The sinister implications of this tendency were masked by euphemisms like "the welfare state", but it soon became evident that the welfare which ensued was subordinate to establishing the supreme control of the State, through registration and later through computerized records, over the lives of individuals. Other essays in this book will undoubtedly deal with the broader aspects of this drawing together of the totalitarian and the "democratic" worlds. Here I will concentrate on the way it has affected the relationship between the arts and the community, and particularly, since this is the area in which I have most experience, on what is happening in 1984 in Canada.

The involvement of the western democracies in the arts came in two stages. First there was the level of communications. When radio came into being the governments of many countries, notably Britain, decided that such a valuable medium of information and opinion, with its virtually unlimited facilities for propaganda, could not be allowed out of the hands of the State. The British Broadcasting Corporation was established in 1927 with monopoly control over radio and later television, and even though independent television was allowed in 1952 and independent local stations in 1970, the major broadcasting channels remained in the control of a State corporation. Theoretically the BBC had an "arm's length" relationship with the government and was free of direct ministerial control, but in practice, during World War II, it became a propaganda service hardly distinguishable from the Ministry of Information; working in its studios George Orwell learnt much about the systematic distortion of truth which he later portrayed in *Nineteen Eighty Four*.

The Canadian Broadcasting Corporation was founded in 1936, largely based on the BBC. From the beginning the Canadian system was a hybrid one, imitating the British with its public network and the Americans with its parallel system of licensed private stations. Again, the CBC was a crown corporation, theoretically independent of government control, but in practice amenable to pressure at times when the reigning administration might feel it necessary for certain policies to be emphasized.

It was this need to gain control over communications as an indispensable aid to modern rulers in spreading information and propaganda that led western governments like those of Britain and Canada into their first involvement in the arts. At first it was a matter of employment rather than real patronage. To keep the attention of the people, the government broadcasting systems had not merely to inform and cajole, but also to entertain, and from the beginning entertainment spanned all the categories from non-art through pop-art to high art. There is no doubt that in Canada, a barren land culturally in the 1930s and even the 1940s, the CBC did help many writers, actors and musicians to survive while in some way or another carrying on their crafts. Until live theatre was revived during the 1950s, it was the CBC that kept going a dramatic tradition with its radio plays, which employed writers, actors and producers and sustained the profession that would later blossom in the independent theatres. Much that happened in this period, however, was due to the enthusiasms of individuals rather than to corporate policy. Robert Weaver, in particular, provided a market in CBC programmes for short stories when neither magazines nor publishers in Canada would take the risk of printing them and he ran programmes that kept criticism alive when there were few journals to give critics space.

But Weaver was operating in the interstices of a vast edifice, and writers who became involved on a broader level, in writing plays and documentaries to slot into set hours and series, found themselves subjected to corporate requirements and the limitations of the medium. How these factors affected their work is shown by the disproportion between the number of plays put on the air and the number that turned out to be capable of adaptation for the theatre or for publication. About ten years ago it was estimated that there were 4,000 radio plays in the CBC archives, which to my knowledge are incomplete in their coverage of what was actually produced, but no more than 100 of these have got into print, and even fewer have been adaptable for the stage.

The CBC, in other words, paid writers to produce what suited its corporate needs; it did not, except in very limited areas like the short story, encourage them to write according to their inclinations. And this situation gave a foretaste of what the writer's situation would be if he became in any real way the pensioner of the State. He might be kept alive, but his talents would be steadily suffocated. Many writers who became highly successful at turning out acceptable work for the CBC were in the end good for nothing else. That is one way of suffocating art. There are others, as we shall see.

Direct patronage, as a function of the modern State rather than of mediaeval corporations, feudal lords or Baroque princes, appeared in the western democracies about a generation ago. It was bred of a notion they shared with — if they did not actually borrow from — the totalitarians, that a nation's arts are the most reliable signs of its nature, and that they are therefore political tokens. To support them, in the hope of manipulating them, may well serve the interests of those in power.

In a small way this was recognized in Britain by the foundation of the British Council in 1936 to introduce the arts abroad through exhibitions and tours by writers. The British Council had little in the way of a patronage role, except that it occasionally paid a writer's fare on a trip he could turn to some literary purpose. Direct patronage began in 1945, when the Committee for the Encouragement of Music and the Arts, which had been set up in 1940 to organize concerts, exhibitions and dramatic performances during the war, was transformed into the Arts Council of Great Britain and endowed with government funds to continue supporting the performing arts and eventually to make grants to individual artists.

Just as the CBC had been modelled on the BBC, so the Canada Council, founded in 1952, was modelled on the Arts Council of Great Britain. It was established, like the CBC, as a Crown Corporation, and theoretically it was independent of government control, though it fell into the sphere of responsibility first of the Secretary of State and then of the Department of Communications.

In the early days the Canada Council did appear, more successfully than the CBC, to resist political pressures. But with the advent of the Trudeau government in 1968 the idea of giving a political direction to the arts began to emerge. At a little publicized seminar held at Ste. Adèle, Québec, in May 1969 and organized by the Canadian Council of the Arts in collaboration with the Associated Councils of the Arts in the United States, some two hundred and fifty arts bureaucrats — and not a single creative artist — gathered to discuss "the political realities of government support of the arts." Both Trudeau and Gérard Pelletier, then Secretary of State, turned up.

Trudeau disarmingly remarked:

"I do not think that modern society, or the artist as a member of that society, need fear a generous policy of subsidy to the arts by governments as long as these governments have the courage to permit free expression and experimentation — and, for that matter, to take it in good part if the mirror held up to their faces is not always a flattering one."

But at the same time he admitted the intention of his government to set "a general course for development" in its aid to the arts and also granted that even so vague a policy could affect the artist's situation.

Pelletier's remarks at the same conference on the "democratization of culture" made it clear that he was considering not the libertarian virtue but the political advantage of developing arts that would appeal to the masses, and Duncan Cameron, then National Director of the government-subsidized Canadian Conference of the Arts, an organization corralling many voluntary groups, talked of the "national organization of the arts" as "an experimental means of achieving the goals essential to the health of the arts and the flourishing of creative expression", and referred to the "total arts community, or arts industry, as it is more commonly now being called." The phrase, "total arts community", suggests of course something monolithic, on the verge of totalitarian, and the phrase "arts industry" clearly indicates the desire to treat works of art as commodities.

For several years the ideas expressed at the Ste. Adèle seminar seemed to lie dormant, but in 1977 the government began to earmark some of its grants to the Canada Council as "thrust funds" tied to prescribed purposes, and in 1978 tried to bring the Council directly into politics by inviting it to propose projects that would "contribute to national unity". The ominous implications of such moves were explored by Frank Milligan, who resigned as the Council's Associate Director, in an essay, "The Ambiguities of the Canada Council", included in David Helwig's symposium: *Love and Money: The Politics of Culture* (1980). If on the whole the Canada Council has up to now proved resistant to efforts to turn it into a quasi-propagandist agency, recent policy documents of the Ministry of Communications display a deliberate intent of confusing communications and "cultural development", which clearly includes the arts, in "policy initiatives" to — in the words of one such document that has come my way — "guarantee that Canadians will produce competitive, world-class products which can reflect our identity and respect our heritage." How long the Council can continue to resist the pressure of politicians and bureaucrats who see the arts as (a) "products" or commodities and as (b) instruments of national politics, and who *control the Council's parliamentary grants,* is clearly problematical.

Even as matters stand, the Council's activities are open to serious criticisms. The greater part of its granting is directed to performing arts, and most of that to supporting institutions, orchestras, theatres, ballet companies — that can be regarded as enhancing the national image, which makes their support a political as much as a cultural act. Comparatively lesser amounts of money go to small groups whose intents are local and grassroots, and only about 16% of the total grants go to individual artists. Here, it is true, the Council has done some good by buying time for artists who might otherwise have found it much more difficult to do their work. But as the competition for grants has grown and funds have become more restricted, the faults of the Council's jury system become evident. Recently I discovered that the average age of jurors for A Grants for writers, which are often sought by people in their 30s with good experimental work to their credit, was 59 and that all the jurors were hall-marked establishment figures. This is hardly what might be regarded as judgement by one's peers, and it has resulted in some notable injustices.

It has seemed to me for a long time that total fairness is impossible within such a system, and I have become convinced that the Canada Council's aid tends to draw the artist into complicity — often unwitting complicity — in a system that at heart is against most of the human and humane values the arts seek to sustain. As Robert Bringhurst recently put the dilemma in *Ocean/Paper/Stone:* "If industry and government rape and prey upon the land — as most certainly they do — can a writer or publisher share in the proceeds without also sharing the crime? And if not, how far back must he stand to regain his innocence." Perhaps the situation is even more compromising for the painters, because of the Council's Art Bank, which buys the works of visual artists of all kinds and then, instead of making them freely available to the people in decentralized galleries, rents them to government offices, so that one can see the works only when visiting bureaucrats, and the art becomes an appendage to the workings of the State.

Despite the recent upsurge in publishing, in the sale of visual art works, in attendance at performing arts events, artists are still the lowest paid class of Canadian workers. Their average income from practising their arts is less than $9,000, and that average takes into account the big earners like Pierre Berton and Toni Onley, the income of most artists is even less than the mean and well below the recognized poverty line. The community owes them a way of increasing their income, but a better method than sporadic grants could be found. The artist would ideally be served by the old Anarchist-Communist solution of the free distribution of goods to fulfill basic needs, or, in a money society, by some kind of guaranteed basic income, applicable to everyone, that would provide for his basic needs and leave him free to produce popular or unpopular art according to his inclinations. But the government has up to now refused even to take the one immediately practicable step that would markedly raise the income of one group of artists as a class: to implement the Public Lending Right that would assure a writer the payments justly due to him for the use of his books by public libraries.

If the Canadian State tempts the artist into complicity with the uncertain offering of the carrots of subsidy, it at the same time tries to bring him to heel by flourishing the stick of taxation. Treating art as a commodity, the Department of National Revenue insists on regarding painters as business men who are to be taxed on their works, regarded as inventory. But other artists, who have to take academic or other jobs because their returns from their work are too small to live on, are treated as hobbyists and not allowed to deduct the expenses for whatever arts they pursue. Musicians performing in symphony orchestras and actors under contract to theatres suddenly find themselves treated as employees, and in the cases of the musicians are not allowed to deduct the cost of the expensive instruments which they have to provide personally. The most absurd case — carrot-and-stick combined — occurred when the Canada Council grant to the Carrousel Theatre was immediately seized by National Revenue because the theatre had not made UIC payments for the actors, whom the taxmen chose to regard as employees. To paraphrase Job, "The state gave and the state hath taken away; blessed be the name of the state!"

There are two ways of destroying free art. One is to censor it out of existence, which the Communists try to do; the other is to tax it out of existence, which seems to be the intent of the Canadian revenue authorities. Either way, it is obviously hoped, the artist will become amenable to the "policy initiatives" of cultural bureaucrats and will "produce competitive, world-class products" for the glory of the nation. On some levels the world of 1984 knows no real frontiers.

ABOUT THE CONTRIBUTORS

Murray Bookchin has been a major spokesperson for more than twenty years for the ecology, appropriate technology and anti-nuclear movements. The author of seven books including *Our Synthetic Environment, Post-Scarcity Anarchism, The Limits of the City, Toward An Ecological Society* and *The Ecology of Freedom,* he lives in Vermont and is Director Emeritus of the Social Ecology Institute.

Noam Chomsky is professor of linguistics at the Massachusetts Institute of Technology. He is author of many books on linguistics and U.S. foreign policy, including most recently *Radical Priorities* (edited by C.P. Otero), *Toward a New Cold War,* the two volume work *The Political Economy of Human Rights* (with Edward S. Herman) and *The Fateful Triangle.*

Yolande Cohen teaches history at the Université du Québec à Montréal. Dr. Cohen edited the collection *Femmes et politique* and has written widely on various aspects of feminism.

Claire Culhane is a long time activist in the peace, human rights and prison abolition movements. She has authored *Why are We in Vietnam?, Barred from Prison* and the forthcoming *Still Barred from Prison.*

John P. Clark teaches philosophy at City College, Loyola University in New Orleans. Dr. Clark has authored several books including *The Philosophical Anarchism of William Goodwin, Max Stirner's Egoism,* and *The Anarchist Moment.*

Jean-Pierre Deslauriers teaches social work at the Université du Québec à Chicoutimi.

Jean Ellezam has taught sociology at several universities. Dr. Ellezam has recently published *Greoupe et Capital:* un nouveau mode social de produire le travail. His forthcoming book is *L'État est Mort.*

Robert Mayo has taught modern languages and comparative literature at Indiana University and the University of North Carolina before joining the faculty of Champlain Regional College in Québec. Dr. Mayo is the author of *Herder and the Beginnings of Comparative Literature.*

Marsha Hewitt is a writer and teaches Humanities and Religious Studies at Vanier College in Montréal. She is co-author of *Their Town* and *One Proud Summer.* An active trade unionist and feminist she is the co-ordinator of the adminstrative committee of the Institut **Anarchos** Institute, and an editor of the journal *Our Generation*.

Dimitrios I. Roussopoulos is an editor, writer, speaker and activist with the peace movement and community-control movements. He has edited seven books on radical social change, and is most recently the author of *The Coming of World War Three*. He is an editor of *Our Generation*, and secretary of the Institut **Anarchos** Institute.

Stephen Schecter teaches sociology at the Université du Québec à Montréal. Dr. Schecter has published *The Politics of Urban Liberation* and *T'es beau en écoeurant*.

George Woodcock is a journalist, poet and author of more than forty books, among them *Ghandi, Dawn and Darkest Hour:* A study of Aldous Huxley, *Canada and Canadians, Anarchism,* and *The Crystal Spirit* (a biography of George Orwell).

The contributors are members of the *Institut* **Anarchos** *Institute.*

more books from

BLACK ROSE BOOKS

write for a free catalogue

THE ANARCHIST MOMENT

Reflections on Culture, Nature and Power

by John Clark

This original contribution to radical social thought attempts for the first time to integrate contemporary philosophical criticism within a framework of ecological concerns and the philosophies of nature.

Arguing for the integration of self, society and nature, Clark finds available social theory inadequate and offers instead a theoretical perspective which combines both Eastern and Western traditions of thought with a radical organicist framework. He speculates that anarchism is capable of being "much more than a noble dream" but is rather "a necessary movement of negation constituting an essential element of the theory of liberation."

Dr. John Clark teaches political science at Loyola University in New Orleans, Louisiana.

220 pages
Paperback ISBN: 0-920057-07-1 $12.95
Hardcover ISBN: 0-920057-08-X $22.95
Philosophy/Politics

LAW AND ANARCHISM

edited by
Thom Holterman and Henc van Maarseveen

"1984 is a good year to read these perceptive essays on law and justice in anarchist thought. Lawyers should read it too... an anarchist understanding of law and its structures must increase the chance that justice will be done, in and out of court."

Clayton Ruby, lawyer

Law and anarchism are usually seen as being diametrical opposites, but in this intriguing collection of essays the editors make the case that anarchism cannot ignore and avoid law and that jurisprudence cannot be disregarded.

The contributors deal with law in a wide sociological sense as the totality of rules of all sorts which exist in a society. Charging that the absolute rejection of law has laid anarchists open to the most absurd charges, the editors have gathered a wealth of reflections on the sources of social authority arising from a revolution based on anarchist principles.

What is the relation between the organized sanction of a self-governing organization and the notion of law? What is the relationship between direct action and the law and how can direct action change the law in such a way as to promote anarchist ideas and the anarchist society?

Contents include: Introduction by Clayton Ruby; Thoughts on an Anarchist Theory of Law and the State; Anarchism and the Theory of Political Law; Anarchism and Legal Rules; Direct Action, Law and Anarchism; Natural Right in the Political Philosophy of P.J. Proudhon; and Kropotkin on Law.

Professors Holterman and van Maarseveen teach at the Faculty of Social Science, Erasmus University, Rotterdam.

216 pages
Paperback ISBN: 0-919619-08-8 $12.95
Hardcover ISBN: 0-919619-10-X $22.95
Law/Philosophy/Politics

OUR GENERATION AGAINST NUCLEAR WAR

edited by
Dimitrios I. Roussopoulos

When the first massive disarmament movement emerged, a journal bearing the title of this book was founded in 1961 to critically examine the issue of war and peace with all its implications. During the following two decades, an extraordinary collection of articles was published covering familiar concerns. Edited by the journal's founding editor, this book contains some of the most insightful and helpful material relevant to today's debate and anti-war movement.

The book includes well documented essays under the following headings: Background Information everyone should know; Spheres of Influence; Canada and the International War System; Unilateralism — what it is?; Neutralism and Non-alignment; Non-violence and Civil Disobedience; Peace Research; the Peace Movement and its Future; Peace, Politics and Philosophy.

Among the many authors of these essays are included: April Carter, Noam Chomsky, Peggy Duff, Eric Fromm, Johan Galtung, Aldous Huxley, Robert Jungk, Michael Klare, Farley Mowat, Seymour Melman, C.B. Macpherson, A.J. Muste, James M. Minifie, Jawaharlal Nehru, Bertrand Russell, Adam Roberts, Ernie Regehr, Gene Sharp, and many others.

477 pages
Paperback ISBN: 0-920057-04-7 $14.95
Hardcover ISBN: 0-920057-15-2 $24.95
Politics/Sociology

DURRUTI: THE PEOPLE ARMED

by Abel Paz

translated by Nancy MacDonald

"...When a column is tired and ready to drop with exhaustion, Durruti goes to talk new courage into the men. When things go bad up Saragossa way, Durruti climbs aboard an aeroplane and drops down in the fields of Aragon to put himself at the head of the Catalonian partisans. Wherever you go it's Durruti and Durruti again, whom you hear spoken of as a wonder-man."
Toronto Daily Star

Forty years of fighting, of exile, of jailings, of living underground, of strikes, and of insurrection, Buenaventura Durruti, the legendary Spanish revolutionary (1896-1936) lived many lives.

Uncompromising anarchist, intransigent revolutionary, he travelled a long road from rebellious young worker to the man who refused all bureaucratic positions, honours, awards, and who at death was mourned by millions of women and men. Durruti believed and lived his belief that revolution and freedom were inseparable.

328, pages, illustrated
Paperback ISBN: 0-919618-74-X $9.95
Hardcover ISBN: 0-919618-73-1 $19.95
History/Labour

RADICAL PRIORITIES

by Noam Chomsky

edited by C.P. Otero

2nd Revised Edition

"...For those who desire a fuller picture of Chomsky's fascinating political scholarship, his **Radical Priorities** *is to be recommended... [it] contains a fine essay on Chomsky by Carlos Otero."*
Harvard International Review

The world-famous linguist at his best. This collection of Noam Chomsky's political writings — the first since 1973 and ignored by the mainstream reviewing media — brings together some of his most important reflections. Many pieces appear for the first time together in English. A broad range of subjects is covered with a view to alerting people about the problems humanity is facing and possible solutions we can undertake.

In the introduction, C.P. Otero lucidly presents an analysis and overview of Chomsky's social and political philosophy unavailable elsewhere. For the first time, the roots of Chomsky's politics are examined in relation to his theory of linguistics.

This book is invaluable for any general reader who would like to make sense out of the daily press. The second revised edition contains new important essays.

Prof. C.P. Otero teaches linguistics at the University of California, Los Angeles.

481 pages
Paperback ISBN: 0-920057-17-9 $14.95
Hardcover ISBN: 0-920057-16-0 $25.95
Politics/Philosophy/Sociology

TOWARD AN ECOLOGICAL SOCIETY

by Murray Bookchin

"Murray Bookchin may be the orneriest political theorist alive... he's worth arguing with... Bookchin is capable of penetrating finely indignant historical analyses... (This book) is another stimulating, wide-ranging collection... (with) several excellent essays on urban planning, the future of the city, new developments in ecologically sound technology, and the history of utopian thought..."
In These Times

"...Murray Bookchin... explains his commitment to an ecology movement based on direct democracy and direct action... just published in Britain."
City Limits

"A revolution needs a prophet, the green revolution no less than others, and there is no shortage of aspirants. Now there are a few names on the lists: Petra Kelly, Rudolf Bahro — and Murray Bookchin... (This) collection of essays... are brilliant and exciting exercises..."
Resurgence

"(This book) is always a provocative work that gives abundant evidence of its author's position at the center of debate... It therefore deserves the careful attention of anyone seriously interested in constructive social thought... It is a work of crucial importance."
Telos

In this exciting new collection of essays, which will stand beside Bookchin's well-known classic, *Post-Scarcity Anarchism* (with its seven printings, translated into five languages), the author deals with all dimensions of social ecology.

320 pages
Paperback ISBN: 0-919618-98-7 $12.95
Hardcover ISBN: 0-919618-99-5 $22.95
Ecology/Philosophy

THE POLITICS OF URBAN LIBERATION

by Stephen Schecter

A broad-ranging study which covers the political economy of the urban question and the importance of the city in the history of social revolution. Prof. Schecter provides the reader with an original evaluation of libertarian insurgency during this century in various countries and urban struggles. The importance of movements from below dealing with housing, transportation and other issues of daily life are contrasted to classical upheavals.

Table of Contents:
Chapter One: The Political Economy of the Urban Question — monopoly capital and the transformation of social life. The fiscal crisis of the state.

Chapter Two: Urban Politics and the Redefinition of the Revolutionary Project — the strategic implications of urban struggles and their contradictions. Libertarian socialism: The material and political possibilities.

Chapter Three: Revolution From Below: The Historical Experience.

Chapter Four: Revolution From Below: Contemporary Urban Struggles — Chile, France, Italy.

Chapter Five: Elements of a Socialist Strategy and the Urban Question.

Chapter Six: The Experience of the MCM.

Chapter Seven: The Impossible Revolution and its Historical Necessity.

240 pages
Paperback ISBN: 0-919618-78-2 $9.95
Hardcover ISBN: 0-919618-79-0 $19.95
Urban Studies/Politics

THE POLITICS OF OBEDIENCE

The Discourse of Voluntary Servitude

by Etienne de la Boétie

"...The Discourse cannot be assimilated into or comprehended as a part of any of the many traditions of political and social thought...It is highly original."
                                            Telos

This classic work of political reflection seeks the answer to the question of why people submit to the tyranny of governments. La Boétie laid the groundwork for the concept of civil disobedience with his proposal that people could cut the bonds of habit and corruption that keep them obedient and complacent, and resolve to serve their masters no more. *The Discourse of Voluntary Servitude* has exerted an important influence on the tradition of pacifism and civil disobedience from Thoreau and Ralph Waldo Emerson, to Tolstoy, to Gandhi.

Etienne de la Boétie was a sixteenth century political philosopher and a close friend of Montaigne.

88 pages
Paperback ISBN: 0-919618-57-X $9.95
Hardcover ISBN: 0-919618-58-8 $19.95
Philosophy/Sociology

THE KRONSTADT UPRISING

by Ida Mett

with a preface by Murray Bookchin

2nd edition

The full story at last of the monumental 1921 events: the first workers' uprising against the Soviet bureaucracy. This book contains hitherto unavailable documents and a bibliography.

93 pages
Paperback ISBN: 0-919618-13-8 $3.45
Hardcover ISBN: 0-919618-19-7 $9.45
History/Politics

THE BOLSHEVIKS AND WORKERS' CONTROL 1917-1921

by Maurice Brinton

Workers' control is again widely discussed and widely researched. This book has two main aims. It seeks to contribute new factual material to the current discussion on workers' control. And it attempts a new kind of analysis of the fate of the Russian Revolution. The two objectives, as will be shown, are inter-related.

100 pages
Paperback ISBN: 0-919618-69-3 $5.95
Hardcover ISBN: 0-919618-70-7 $12.95
History/Politics

THE CUBAN REVOLUTION

A Critical Perspective

by Sam Dolgoff

This book sheds new light on the Cuban revolution. It also adds new dimensions to the traditional way in which fundamental social and political changes take place. Until the publication of this book the interpretation of the significance of the Cuban revolution and its development has been dominated by conservative, liberal and Marxist scholars or observers. These commentators have been either highly critical, apologetic, or have attempted to write an "objective" assessment. In every case they have ignored major segments of the history of Cuba.

275 pages
Paperback ISBN: 0-919618-35-9 $9.95
Hardcover ISBN: 0-919618-36-7 $19.95
Latin American Studies/History/Politics

THE UNKNOWN REVOLUTION 1917-1921

by Voline

This famous history of the revolution in Russia and its aftermath has been long out of print. The present edition combines the previous two-volume English-language edition plus omitted material from later editions. It is a complete translation of *La Révolution inconnue*, first published in French in 1947, and republished in Paris in 1969 by Editions Pierre Belfond.

717 pages, illustrated
Paperback ISBN: 0-919618-25-1 $9.95
Hardcover ISBN: 0-919618-26-6 $20.95

LOUISE MICHEL

by Edith Thomas

translated by Penelope Williams

"Although the Commune remains a controversial phenomenon, one of its best-known figures, Louise Michel, won great sympathy in almost all quarters. ...the woman was sui generis and matches the legend because of her courage, her limitless generosity, and her singleminded devotion to the cause she made hers..."

American Historical Review

Revolutionary on the barricades of the Paris Commune, tried before the War Council of France, deported to a penal colony, received by enthusiastic crowds upon her return, brillant lecturer throughout Europe, continuously followed by the police, participant in spectacular trials and demonstrations, threatened by assassins, imprisoned time and again, Louise Michel, writer, teacher, poet, feminist, is one of the most extraordinary legends in the literature of freedom.

400 pages
Paperback ISBN: 0-919619-07-4 $12.95
Hardcover ISBN: 0-919619-08-2 $22.95
Women/Sociology/History

A PRIMER OF LIBERTARIAN EDUCATION

by Joel Spring

"I find it powerful and liberating... I think this is a very valuable and important book; it has done a great deal to intensify, correct and further radicalize my thoughts."

Jonathan Kozol

"Spring's book is unique. It stands serenely outside the muddy stream of literature spawned by the recent wave of criticism of compulsory schooling. In the midst of papermountains 'pro' and 'con', Spring places the radical challenge into its own tradition of libertarian anarchy, and of concern with law and freedom. This is the only readable book I know which does so in simple language and with the clearsightedness of the competent historian. Students of contemporary education cannot avoid this one."

Ivan Illich

157 pages
Paperback ISBN: 0-919618-61-8 $7.95
Hardcover ISBN: 0-919618-62-6 $17.95
Education/Sociology

Printed by
the workers of
Editions Marquis, Montmagny, Québec
for
Black Rose Books Ltd.